Mission of Honor

A moral compass for a moral dilemma

Dedication

This book is dedicated to the Gold Star Families of the Vietnam War as well as the men that served in that conflict; but especially to 1LT Thomas Francis Shaw who showed me the right path to take in a perilous world.

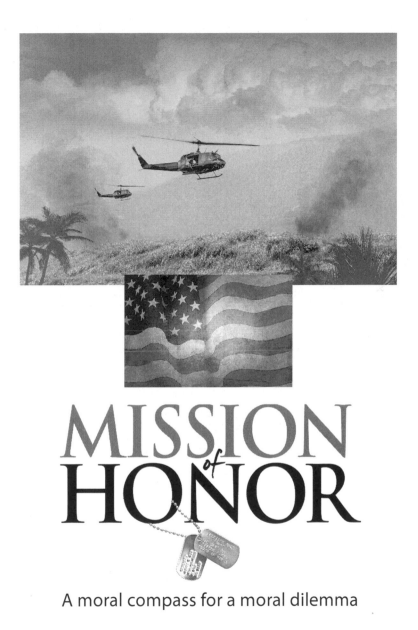

MISSION of HONOR

A moral compass for a moral dilemma

JIM CRIGLER

Mission of Honor

A moral compass for a moral dilemma

First published in 2017 by
Panoma Press Ltd
48 St Vincent Drive, St Albans, Herts, AL1 5SJ UK
info@panomapress.com
www.panomapress.com

Cover design by Michael Inns
Artwork by Karen Gladwell

ISBN 978-1-784521-08-0

A CIP catalogue record for this book is available from the British Library.

This book is available online and in all good bookstores.

CONTENTS

FOREWORD

This book is the story of so many young pilots of that time. It took me back to those days over 40 years ago. We lived day to day in Vietnam, not knowing if we would see the next sunrise or sunset. It was a constant that we all just lived with, and like any combat veterans we continue to live it to some degree every day of our lives.

I first met Jim Crigler at Fort Wolters, Texas in the fall of 1970. We were Warrant Officer Candidates in 1st WOC or the Big Red One. After primary training it was on to Fort Rucker, Alabama for instrument training and transition into the Icon of the Vietnam War, the UH-1 "Huey". We lived through the grueling inspections and verbal abuse designed to separate the strong from the weak. It was like forging steel.

Jim and I were both honored and burdened with the mission of burial escort duty. It changed our lives forever. Seeing and feeling the grief of those special families up close was gut wrenching and it is still part of us both to this day. But it was our honored duty.

The loss of our comrades in arms is ever present in our souls. Their faces will never age as we have done in these 40+ years. These men were our friends, people we ate and drank and laughed and cried with. They were in most cases men that we only knew for a few months or maybe a year. But these were men whom we would die for and they for us. Even today those that survived the war are still the men that we yearn to be around.

All of the men that we flew with in Vietnam took great pride in our accomplishments. For most of us the tempering in fire in both flight school and combat has helped us excel in our lives. But when our time comes and we head to the great hangar in the sky I'm certain that we will be welcomed by and know the faces that will greet us.

Dennis L. Faucher D.D.S.
Ex CW2 Pilot 129th Assault Helicopter Co

Author's Note

Memories don't last forever. After 45 years even the best of memories will dim. In my case to help me remember so far in the past I researched much of my personal correspondence, reviewed all of my personal Vietnam photo collection, tracked down and interviewed most of the pilots, crew chiefs, and gunners that I flew with and did my best to give as accurate a depiction of what happened as possible. If nothing else, it's damned close. But if I did make a mistake please, let me acknowledge in advance that mistakes, like the ones I made in life that I talk about in this book, make good and entertaining stories and often, as is the case in this book, have a lesson to be learned from them.

Also of special note, though I talk mostly about the helicopter pilots in this book, the real heroes of our helicopter crews in Vietnam were the two men in the back of the bird. The crew chiefs and gunners were the men that did all the work and protected us pilots with their brash antics and skillful use of the M60 machine guns. And they did it all while we pilots did our best to learn how to fly in those combat situations. The men in the back of the bird are my true heroes.

Lastly, I have purposely left out or changed a few names where I thought that the statute of limitations on embarrassment had not run out. In the case of my two girlfriends, both of their names have been changed to protect their anonymity and privacy. But the remainder of this book is exactly as I remember it happening.

My Army dog tag and dog tag from American Huey 369.

Prologue

There have been many books written about the Vietnam War. I did not set out to write one of them. For me the war was well behind in my life's rear-view mirror and I had been looking forward in life for many years. But over those years the war kept creeping up on me like a mosquito that keeps buzzing around your ear. It won't go away until it's satisfied with blood or you kill it. For over 40 years I let that mosquito buzz in my head. My life was impacted in so many ways by Vietnam. I focused intently on anything other than that war. I've had trouble in positions that I worked in with authority figures and people that did crazy and stupid acts. I worked beyond extremely hard at every endeavor, whether it was work or play. 80 hour work weeks were the norm for me for many, many years. I even left the corporate world and started my own company because of this mosquito. But always my war would return.

Then a few years ago several of my grandsons asked if I would write some stories or perhaps a book from my time in Vietnam. They had read some books on that war and discovered that

helicopter pilots were key players in every battle. And that was my job. In Vietnam I was a warrant officer helicopter UH-1 Huey pilot. I agreed to try. For six months I would periodically sit down at my computer and try to hammer out my thoughts on the year that I had spent in Vietnam. But only a few stories came to my mind, the rest was blocked out by a brain that had shoved those nasty memories so far in the back of my mind that all I had was a blank slate. Many people that I spoke to on book writing advised me to just start writing. They said it would all come to me. But it did not come to me. I needed to remember what had happened and put it together so that it made sense to me. My mind was still a blank.

Then one December day in 2010, I called up my 82 year old mother to see if she had kept any of my correspondence with her from my time in Vietnam. Indeed she had kept every letter. Some weeks later in January I received an envelope with 12 or 14 letters that I had written and sent to her from Vietnam. They were in a small stack with a piece of yarn tied around them in a bow for keepsake. My mom had obviously kept these letters safe as a memento for over forty years. All of them except one said "Free" where a stamp should have been. I went through the envelopes and organized them by postmark from September 1971 until September 1972 - the time of my tour in Vietnam. But there was one letter left. It was dated December 5th 1972, several months after I came back from Vietnam. Tomorrow morning I will start this journey by reading my words from so long ago.

I live in seclusion at the back of a two hundred acre wooded valley at the end of a one mile road. There is only one way in and one way out. I like it that way. On this early January morning there was a foot of snow in the valley and the snowflakes were still coming down. It was not yet dawn as I started a fire in the fireplace. My wife and two youngest daughters were still asleep. On this snowy morning I would read those letters and commence writing my thoughts on paper. I poured a cup of coffee and sat in front of the fire and grabbed the stack of letters. I decided to start from the back forward so I grabbed the letter dated December 5th 1972. I was curious why this letter was even in the stack to begin with. But as I viewed this letter my heart sank as I read the words of a very distraught young man. This letter was a suicide note that I had written to my mother in a fit of despair. I did not remember writing this letter. But there it was in plain ink in my own handwriting. I wondered why my mother had kept such a thing. But I read that letter over and over. My stomach churned and my heart ached each time I read it. I could not only remember those memories, I could still feel the pain. It was still there after all these years.

When one reads their own suicide note it has a way of making you sit up straight in your chair. I was now more determined than ever to kill this mosquito. But there was much more to it than that. As a young man, just prior to my experiences in Vietnam, I was boy in trouble. I had a moral dilemma that needed to be solved. This book is about solving that dilemma and finding purpose as well as a true mission in life.

Jim Crigler

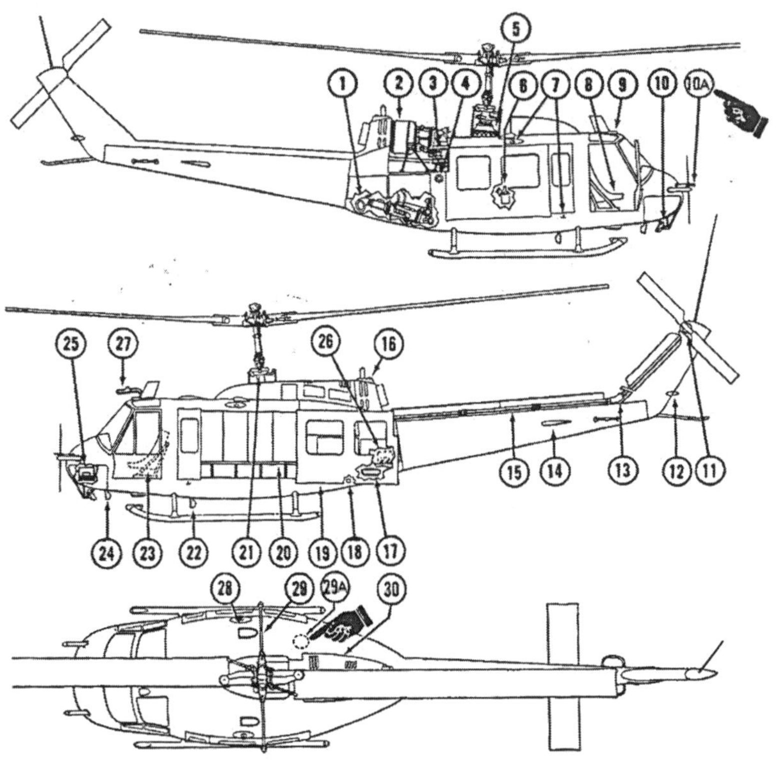

General Arrangement Diagram

1. Heating Burner and Blower Unit
2. Engine
3. Oil Tank Filler
4. Fuel Tank Filler
5. Transmission
6. Hydraulic Reservoir (Pressure Type)
7. Forward Navigation Lights (4)
8. Pilot's Station
9. Forward Cabin Ventilator (2)
10. Cargo Suspension Mirror

10A. Pitot Tube (Nose Mount)

11. Tail Rotor (90o) Gear Box
12. Aft Navigation Light
13. Tail Rotor Intermediate (45o) Gear Box
14. Synchronized Elevator
15. Tail Rotor Drive Shaft
16. Anti-Collision Light
17. Oil Cooler
18. External Power Receptacle
19. Cargo-Passenger Door
20. Passenger Seats Installed
21. Swashplate Assembly
22. Landing Light
23. Copilot's Station
24. Search Light
25. Battery
26. Alternate Battery Location (Armor Protection Kit)
27. Pitot Tube (Roof Mount)
28. Aft Cabin Ventilators (2)
29. Stabilizer Bar

29A. Hydraulic Reservoir (Gravity-feed type)

30. Engine Cowling

■ *Diagrams showing the locations of the exterior Huey assembly*

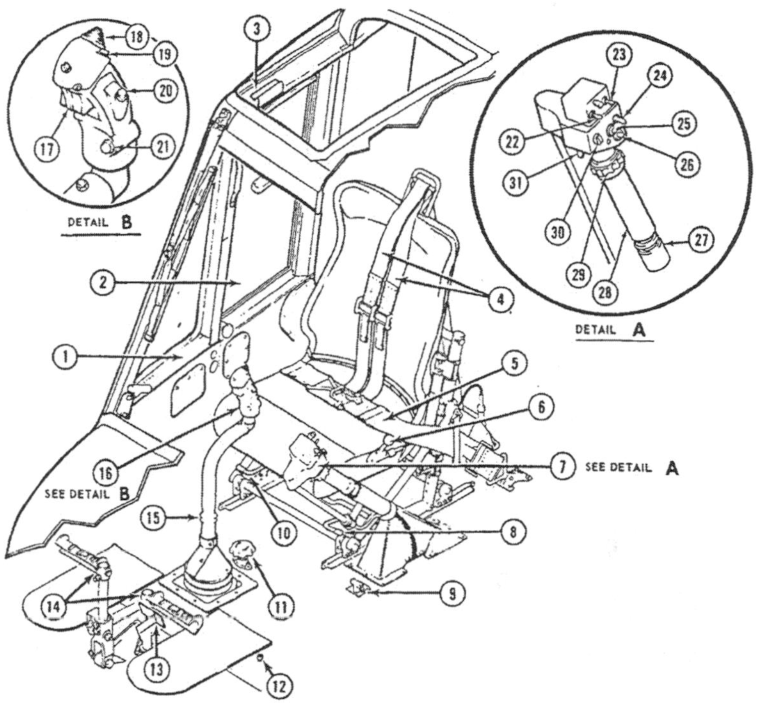

Pilot's station - typical

1. Pilot's Entrance Door
2. Sliding Window Panel
3. Hand Hold
4. Shoulder Harness
5. Seat Belt
6. Shoulder Harness Lock-Unlock Control
7. Collective Pitch Control Lever
8. Seat Adjustment Fore and Aft
9. Collective Pitch Down Lock
10. Seat Adjustment Vertical
11. Directional Control Pedal Adjuster
12. Microphone Foot Switch
13. External Cargo Mechanical Release
14. Directional Control Pedals
15. Cyclic Control Friction Adjuster
16. Cyclic Control Stick
17. Microphone Trigger Switch
18. Hoist Switch
19. Force Trim Switch
20. Armament Fire Control Switch
21. External Cargo Electrical Release Switch
22. Search Light ON-OFF Stow Switch
23. Landing Light ON-OFF Switch
24. Landing Light EXTEND-RETRACT Switch
25. Search Light EXTEND-RETRACT LEFT-RIGHT Control Switch
26. Engine Idle Release Switch
27. Collective Pitch Control Friction Adjuster
28. Power Control (Throttle)
29. Power Control Friction Adjuster
30. Governor RPM INCREASE-DECREASE Switch
31. Starter Ignition Trigger Switch

Diagram showing the locations of the interior Huey assembly

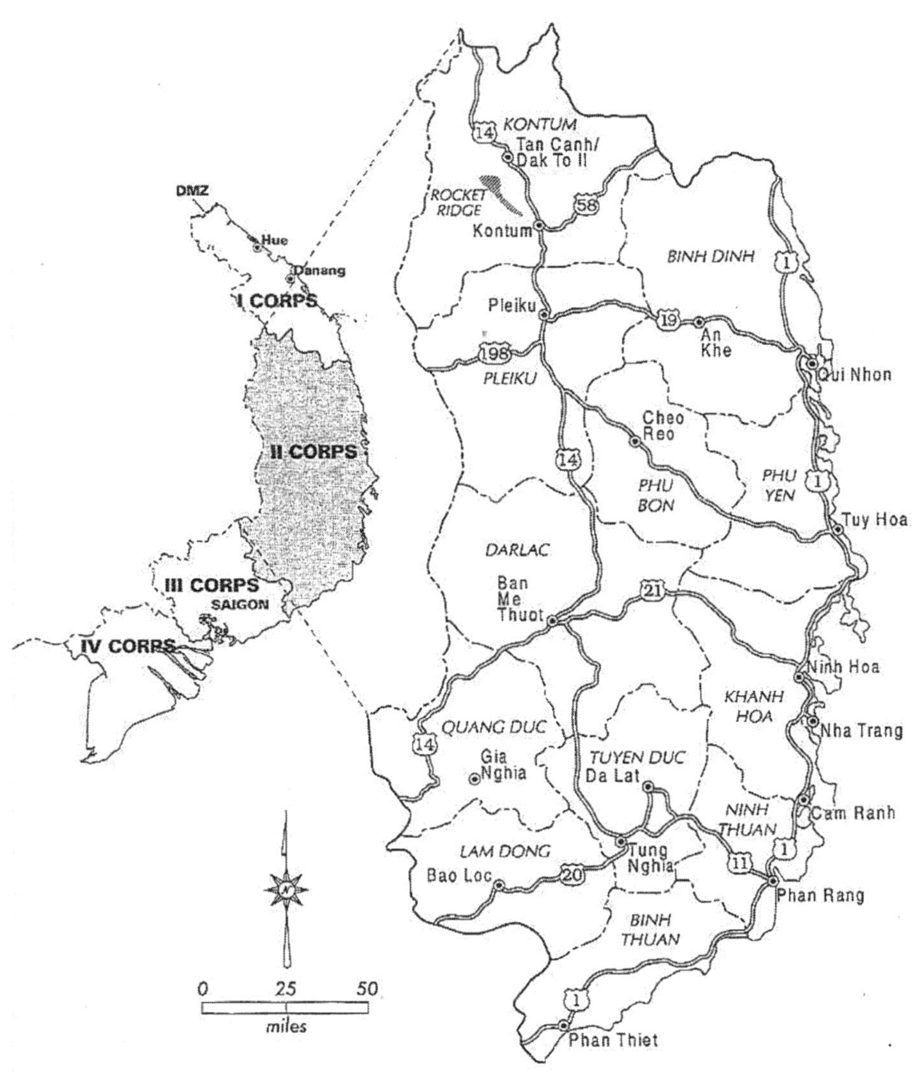

Vietnam II Corps showing major cities, roads, and provinces

CHAPTER ONE:
WE GOTTA GET OUT OF THIS PLACE

Vietnam Central Highlands April 11th, 1972

Augie pressed his mic and said, "Take the aircraft Crigs, I want you to fly the next sortie. We have two more supply runs into An Khe Pass outpost and I need a break."

"Roger, I have the aircraft," I said.

I liked flying as co-pilot with WO1 Augie Bailey. He was a brilliant pilot and an excellent teacher for me in combat. But today was a real shit fest. On our last mission into the An Khe Pass outpost we saw bodies everywhere, including several still stuck in the razor wire from the previous night's assault from the NVA (North Vietnamese Army). We took small arms fire on almost every approach into that outpost. I flew low down the mountain side to our resupply pickup point. We loaded up with mortars, night flares, ammo and water. The Korean RTO (Radio Translation Operator) advised us that sporadic mortar fire had been taken at the An Khe Pass outpost since we left. The Korean company commander did not want us to land on the helipad but rather hover directly over his base and drop off the supplies. He needed that ammo desperately.

Augie looked at me and said, "Screw that hover stuff! When you fly back in Crigs I want you to be at a hover but moving forward as the RTO and Crew dump everything out the back. It won't be pretty but we will get them their supplies."

"Got it," I said.

I flew back up the mountainside and low level along the ridge. I did not do a textbook approach but kind of a hot flare into the middle of the outpost. I almost hit the tail of the Huey on a radio antenna as I flared. There were no Koreans in sight as they were all hunkered down in their foxholes. This was not a good sign.

"Alright, get that stuff thrown out the back," Augie yelled in his mic. "Crigs, keep it moving forward."

Just then I heard a 'whoomph' as a mortar round hit somewhere behind us.

"Keep moving Crigs," Augie said.

"Sir this place is going really hot!" said SP4 Gary Woodward, the crew chief.

'Whoomph, whoomph' went two additional mortars.

"All out!" said Woodward.

"Crigs, get us the hell out of here!" shouted Augie.

I pulled pitch and nosed the Huey over to gain airspeed. We were in and out of that outpost within six seconds.

"That was close," I said.

"You did well Crigs," said Augie.

"Well I'm glad you didn't notice how scared shitless I was!" I said.

Augie laughed, "That's what it's like when you dance with the devil, Jim!"

"Dance with the devil?" I thought, "How the hell did I ever end up in this place?"

"Sir, can we put on some tunes?" asked Woodward.

"Sure" Augie said as he tuned in the ADF Radio to AFVN.

Automatic Direction Finder Radio was an AM radio that we used to hone in on a beacon to use for flight location reference. AFVN was the AM station that stood for Armed Forces Vietnam and they played the most popular music of the day.

Eric Burdon and the Animals were singing "We Gotta Get Out Of This Place". The whole crew started singing that song out loud - I'm sure the Korean RTO thought we were all nuts. All we thought was "we gotta get out of this place!"

Chapter Two:

We All Start Somewhere

"A young man needs direction in life...
and sometimes mentorship.

When that is absent his life can be like
a feather in the wind."

I was born the second son of Jim and Flo Crigler on February 2nd, 1950. My older brother, also named James, died shortly after childbirth in what was known at the time as "Crib Death". Perhaps their determination to name me James as well meant something special. I eventually became the eldest of nine children. My father was a real dreamer and was always starting new business ventures. Until I was 12 I thought my mom was permanently pregnant. With an ever growing family we were constantly relocating from one house to another and always changing schools. Our family life was anything but stable. My dad worked in construction which was booming in the 1950s. He was Builder of the Year in 1958 when I was eight years old. By the time I was nine years old he was bankrupt. We moved from a nice house in a brand new subdivision to a rental home with no running water. My parents would constantly argue and dad was a real drunk during this period of my life. My dad and mom had hit bottom and we kids were right there with them. Though my parents did their best, we rarely had enough room, or food, or money.

My parents often would drop me and my brother Mike at my mother's parents. Frank and Florence Feltmeier were wonderful people. Frank worked for Pittsburgh Paints for 35 years and they had lived in the same house since the 1920s. Florence was a devout Catholic and homemaker who attended mass daily. Mike and I spent most weekends and many summers helping my grandparents with their mowing, gardening, tree trimming, and everything else you can imagine. In the summer Frank would show me and Mike how to plant tomatoes, trim fruit trees, and the wonders of squishing peppermint leaves between your fingers and that fantastic smell that lingered on your hands until you washed. He would take us everywhere and we saw how outspoken and confident he was in life. And we watched him smoke cigarettes. Frank usually smoked about 3 packs a day. We would also sit together on many a summer evening and listen to Harry Cary announce the Cardinals baseball game on KMOX Radio. He was content with me and Mike and we were content with him.

My grandparents were also a World War II "Gold Star" family, having lost their youngest son Bill on the beaches of Tarawa in the South Pacific. In November 1943 Bill Feltmeier was one of the thousands of Marines that died in that battle. Every day that we stayed with them my grandmother would wake us up for 7:30am mass at St Rita's Catholic Church. It was the most stable part of my life. In the summer months we would help Grandma make jams and can tomatoes and other fruits and vegetables. We would stir and lick the pots clean. She would walk around the kitchen helping us, focusing on whatever recipe we were preparing. Florence was a real character of life. Occasionally she would cut a fart and we would all get a good laugh. She would always say something like, “There’s more room out than there is in” or “never trust a woman that does not fart!”.

Going home from Grandma’s at the end of those summers was always hectic and frenzied. More kids, another house, Dad’s new job and there was never enough room. It was a very chaotic home life. My mom, like my grandmother Florence, was a staunch catholic. My father never attended mass except for weddings and funerals. But the influence by my mother and grandmother towards the Church was strong. In fact, so much so that later in my early teens I had interest in the priesthood. My Grandmother was always telling me what a great priest I would make.

Several years later at a retreat at a St. Louis Seminary for potential priests I ended my desires for the priesthood. I had asked one of the priests during a discussion about celibacy how difficult it was for him to stay celibate. He said it was “God’s calling for him” and that I would have a sign if it was for me. Later that day during mass I had one of those teenage uncontrollable erections that just would not go away. It was my sign. I would not pursue the priesthood. I am grateful for my grandparents’ influence. But I was not old enough to ask my grandfather about the tougher questions in life. I’m sure he would have been “straight to the point” and given me clear mentorship instructions. But that was not to be. He died in November 1963 just a few days after President John F. Kennedy was killed in Dallas, Texas. His cigarette habit had finally taken its toll. I was 13 years old. I still miss my grandfather to this day.

An Absent Father

My dad continued to start new businesses, never quite reaching what he set out to do. They always seemed to fail at the wrong time. Once in 1962 when I was 12 years old we were so broke that my mom went to the Church for help. I'm not sure whether my grandmother had any pull with the priests but a parish in Kirkwood Missouri, St Peters, put us up in an abandoned Carmelite Nuns' convent located at 109 Geyer Road. It was a godsend for my parents and for us nine kids it was a paradise.

The convent had 10 bedrooms and an eight foot high wooden fence surrounding three full acres. We lived there for about 18 months while my dad got back on his feet. During that time I played in the large yard, attended St Peter's Catholic School and was an altar boy at mass many weekdays. I turned 13 in that convent and it was also my first attempt at work. I sold Sunday papers on a busy corner on Geyer Road and later worked at St Joseph's Hospital cleaning floors. My dad was always gone, whether he was working or not. We saw him on weekends. I'm not sure how many jobs he had during this period but apparently there were a lot. He also drank a lot as well. I suppose the pressure to provide for a wife and nine children was pretty overwhelming. And my dad was overwhelmed.

Hauling Hay

In 1963 we moved to Jackson, Missouri. My dad had gotten a job through my grandfather and was working for Pittsburgh Plate Glass in Cape Girardeau, Missouri. Jackson was a small farming town with a population of about five thousand. It was six miles away from Cape Girardeau. This was a big change from St. Louis for my brothers and sisters. But we loved it.

The thing about moving every year or two is that you have to learn how to make friends quickly. And we all did. My new friends were sons of farmers or daughters of workers at the Brown Shoe Factory down the street. And amazingly, my mother was able to find a house almost as big as the nun convent. She met an aging old man that had an eight bedroom house for rent. His name was Mr. Mueller and he was the youngest of nine children. When he met my mom and all nine of us kids he just had to have us live in his rental house. He charged us $100.00 per month and insisted that we stay as long as we wanted. It was great living in that town. On weekends we would go hunting on the various farms. No pigeon was safe around us. And we knew where every covey of quail hid out. We also worked on the farms, especially during the summer hay season. The farmers would make thousands of small 60 to 70 pound hay bales and they needed them picked off the fields, hauled to the barn and stacked for the winter. We earned a dollar an hour or three cents a bale, whichever was greater. Three cents a bale was usually the winner.

I liked working for those farmers. They showed me the meaning of work and it was a great way to work outdoors and stay in shape. But it wasn't all work. Though we would start at 7am, there was usually an hour to hour and a half break around lunchtime. The farmer's wife would set out a spread of food on the table that would rival any holiday meal that I had known. There was fried chicken, ham, potatoes, coleslaw, and all the lemonade you could drink. And there was always cake or pie for dessert. And immediately after the meal every teenager would plop down on the grass for a quick nap. Then, back to work until sundown lifting and hauling thousands of bales in the afternoon. It was perfect country comradery and by August all of us were in great shape. I knew now why all the country boys on our football team were so strong.

It was now 1964 and the Vietnam War was just coming on the news scene as a regular topic. But at 14 years old I had other distractions. The Beatles rock group from England was just coming on the music scene. I was an instant fan. In fact, I was the first kid at Jackson High School to wear a Beatles haircut. My dad hated it. He also did NOT like the Beatles. He was a solid Country and Western fan and the Beatles did not fit well with him. As my hair got longer my dad got more disgusted. As he traveled all week, it was the weekends that I had to endure his wrath. But my hair continued to grow. Finally, my dad had enough. He sat me down for a haircut and put a bowl on my head. He said, "if you are going to comb your hair down instead of up then we are going to make it easier to cut." And boy did I look silly. But I was so angry with him that I just left it the way he cut it. On Monday I went to school and was an instant sensation! The girls loved it. Suddenly I was a pretty popular guy at school.

Football Star in a Small Town

We lived in that house in Jackson, Missouri longer than anyplace else: about four and a half years.

I went to three different schools in Jackson; Immaculate Conception Catholic School, Jackson Junior High and Jackson Senior High. During my sophomore and junior years I played football for the Jackson High Indians. I loved it. Being on the team meant wearing your letter jacket in school. The guys on the football team were the "big men on campus" and had a lot of prestige, especially on game day. We played all over Southeast Missouri at towns like Cape Girardeau, Poplar Bluff, Perryville, and Sikeston.

The team was a close knit group led by coach Tim Lee. Coach Lee was one of those ex-college lineman football players that had no neck. He was all muscle. We all loved Coach Lee.

I came into my own at football in the fall of 1966. While President Lyndon Johnson was talking about escalating the war in Vietnam and committing another hundred thousand troops, I was playing offensive and defensive halfback for the Jackson High Indians. And I was pretty good at it. I was also looking forward to playing my senior year, knowing if I got good enough I might just qualify for a football scholarship to a college in the area. I even had my first crush on a girl named Vicky Gibbs.

CHAPTER THREE:

BIG CITY SCHOOL - CHAOS IN 1968

The fall of 1966 was a great year for me in high school. By now I had lettered in both football and track. I was one of the top players on our team and it really felt good to wear that letter jacket as I walked down the halls of Jackson High school. But as luck and life would have it, my dad decided to get a new job which required relocation back to St. Louis. By January 1967, half way through my junior year, we had moved to Hazelwood, Missouri. We went from a huge eight bedroom home on three acres to a three bedroom ranch house on a postage stamp size lot. Our landlord in Jackson, Mr. Mueller, was devastated. So were my brother Mike and I. At school we went from a small high school with about five hundred students to Hazelwood High which operated in two shifts of 2000 students each. And there also wasn't nearly enough room in that house for the 11 of us. So Mike and I built a room in the basement out of moving boxes.

It was tough transitioning to Hazelwood. We had no friends except those we might meet on the bus to school. I had a letter of recommendation from Coach Lee that I took to the football coach at Hazelwood. Coach Lee had done a good job in the letter talking about my stamina and ability to play both offensive and defensive positions during the same game. I was pretty proud to hand that letter over to the coach at Hazelwood. I thought for sure he would invite me on the team or at least to try out. I don't remember his name but he was a big muscle of a guy, taller than Coach Lee but had the same "No Neck" appearance of a college football lineman. He looked at the letter, looked at me, and then looked at the letter again.

"Sorry Jim, I can't use you," he said, "You're just too small. I'm sure that in your smaller high school football division you were fine but here I can only use the big guys. Otherwise we get slammed on the field."

Then he handed the letter back to me and said, "You should go out for track."

I walked out of that office as dejected as could be. There went my opportunity for football scholarship. I decided not to go out for track either. I made up my mind to settle in to my new school and just make the best of it. Hazelwood High for me was more like a warehouse. Two shifts of students and hardly any homework. In fact I don't remember having *any* homework. This was very different from Jackson High where teachers pushed us to learn and we always had homework. I guess for the teachers at Hazelwood it was enough to just survive the class sizes much less grade lots of homework.

Vietnam Tet Offensive 1968

Throughout my senior year at Hazelwood High School the Vietnam War blew up on television. President Johnson continued to send more and more troops into combat. Then in January

1968 the North Vietnamese and the Viet Cong forces launched an offensive with 70,000 troops attacking throughout South Vietnam. The attack occurred on the Vietnamese New Year called "Tet" and the press quickly dubbed the battle the "Tet Offensive". Thousands were killed on both sides. But the North Vietnamese got the worst of it with more than 10 times the casualties of the Americans. The United States had soundly defeated the North whose military operations were now in shambles. The Viet Cong or VC never fully recovered after the Tet Offensive and it took the North Vietnamese until the spring of 1972 to recover.

But the tide also turned with the American public and now a bigger anti-war sentiment was prevalent in the U.S., so the North Vietnamese had won a public relations victory. The Paris peace talks just continued to drag on. It was now very obvious that the American public was getting tired of the Vietnam War. Even so there were still patriotic young men willing to serve. I knew many guys in high school that signed up for various spots in the Army, Navy, Marines, and the Air Force. Many even joined before graduating high school. During high school I personally had no thought of joining the military service as I wanted to be the first in my family to get a college degree. But one thing WAS on the minds of all the young men that were about to graduate; the "draft". Many of the men that joined did so to avoid being drafted into the Army or Marines which were considered the "bullet stopper" jobs, whereas, in general, the Navy and Air Force were considered safer positions. At least this was the sentiment at my high school. Not everyone planned on going to college. And if you did not have a college deferment or a physical disability that would keep you from serving after you graduated high school you were subject to being drafted. At 18 years old we were all required by law to register for the draft.

Martin Luther King

I was pretty astute at the national news for an 18 year old. I had a keen interest in the Freedom Marches that Dr. Martin Luther King conducted. I had never seen the type of racism that nightly news talked about in the Southern United States and it intrigued me that Dr. King was using Gandhi's peaceful non-violent method of protest. We had learned about Gandhi's revolution in high school and I was in awe that we were now seeing the same thing in the United States. But it all ended in April of 1968 when Dr. King was murdered in Memphis. It seemed like chaos would continue during my entire senior year.

A Girl to Fall in Love With

I had never had a steady girlfriend up until this point in my life. Then I met a young girl named Diane Pastors on a double date. Man did I fall head over heels for this girl. We did everything together. Drive in movies on Friday nights, date night to the indoor theater, and just meeting at the local hang out to talk. A favorite was hanging out at the local Steak & Shake. Everyone would drive their muscle cars through the lot and around the circle before they would find a spot to park for some fries and a cherry coke. It was always fun hanging out with Diane. Unfortunately, Diane's parents were going through some tough times. Her mother was a pretty bad alcoholic and would constantly be drunk on vodka. I'm not sure whether they just thought I was not the right guy for their daughter or the booze clouded their judgment but they let it be known that Diane was not available. They restricted her to the house, did not let her drive the car. And they screened all the phone calls that I made to her. But we still met anyway. I even asked her to my senior prom at high school. We just could not stay away from each other. The more her parents restricted us, the more we tried to get together.

High School Graduation

In May of 1968 I graduated high school. Having no idea what I wanted to do next, except go to college, I sat with my parents to talk about how to finance my schooling. They were adamant that there was no money for college. My dad repeatedly told me, "You don't need college son, just look at me."

Frankly, I did look at him. That was a big reason that my heart was set on getting a college degree. But without money that left me only one alternative: go out and work and make enough to pay for it myself.

Robert Kennedy is Assassinated June 1968

I quickly found work at a local car wash and gas station repair shop. I was making 2 dollars and 25 cents an hour and I was pretty excited. I even bought a used car. It was a 1966 red GTO convertible. It had 3 deuces (two barrel carburetors), a 389 cubic inch engine and a four speed transmission. So much for college savings. Then, in June, more chaos for the country. Robert Kennedy was assassinated while campaigning in California. This was pretty upsetting to me as I was not able to vote as an 18 year old, but if I could have voted, Bobby Kennedy would have been my choice. I was old enough to be drafted and fight a war but not old enough to vote. (Three years later, in March of 1971, Congress would change the law to give 18 year olds the right to vote.) Bobby Kennedy was the third assassination in five years in the United States. The Vietnam War continued to escalate.

CHAPTER FOUR:
DRAFT BAIT

I worked as much as I could during the summer of 1968. I would wash 30 cars a day, pump gas for the customers that would drive up to the pumps, and help the main mechanic, Jim Stubbs. You didn't talk back to Jim Stubbs. If he told you to do something you better well get it done or you got the wrath of Jim. He would not put up with any slackers. I would regularly work 60 to 70 or more hours a week across 6 days. It was exhausting work and I relished my Saturday night dates with Diane. Sundays I usually slept most of the day. Then starting on Monday I would do it all over again. Between car, insurance, and gas I had little left to save for college. But still living at home in a room made of boxes in the basement meant I had no rent. That helped. At the end of the summer my parents once again moved, this time to southwest St. Louis County to the town of Manchester. This made it much more difficult for me to get to work but it was still cheaper than renting an apartment. For a year I worked and commuted. By the end of that year I had a total of $300.00 saved up for college. Not enough to get me into any university but enough to start out at a junior college. Meramec Junior College was $125.00 per semester plus books.

College Fall 1969

It was now 1969 and I started the fall semester at Meramec. I had now gotten a job working part time at Spirit of St. Louis Airport in Chesterfield, MO. It was a lot closer to home and very convenient for school. Plus I was able to learn a lot about flying. I even got a ride with the local State Patrol helicopter which I often refueled.

College was a totally different experience than high school. There was homework, and lots of it. And my classes were made up of students that had just graduated high school and military veterans. There were lots of veterans going to school on the GI Bill.

Chapter Five:
The Times They Are a Changing

Vietnam in the News: War Protests

The Vietnam War was everywhere. Life magazine, Time magazine, every newspaper, and every nightly news program carried the war. It was impossible to get away from it and anti-war protests would take place everywhere. There were large marches on Washington, D.C. and it seemed like every major city had a protest march. Ever since the Democratic Convention in 1968 in Chicago and the subsequent rioting, the protests just continued to escalate. And nowhere was there more discussion and change taking place than on college campuses. After the first couple of weeks at college I settled into a routine. I would go to my classes. Then go to the student union to have a Coke and study as much as I could. Then I would make it to work for whatever shift I had that day. Often it was the 3pm to 11pm shift. Gradually, I noticed more dissent on the Meramec campus and the war protests got more visible as well, especially in the late winter and spring when the weather warmed in St. Louis. In the outdoor common areas there were often public debates staged, with many students opposing the war and veterans taking a position supporting the war. These talks got very heated and at times I thought that fights would break out. Though fists never flew there were a lot of demeaning comments made and many feelings hurt on both sides. The veterans, most of whom had joined the service, tried to justify their opinions. But it seemed like neither side budged. Our campus was as divided as our country was about Vietnam.

I made friends with many of the veterans on campus, especially many of those that were in my classes. I was also friends with many of those that were opposed to the war. Many times I was asked to join protests and burn my draft card. I never did. I thought the veterans on campus were pretty good about those protests. They had done their duty and now they were allowing the freedom of speech they served for to play out. I never saw a veteran publicly get angry at draft card burning protests. In the spring of 1970 the country was on fire.

Vietnam Veterans on Campus

Most of the veterans on campus were not combat veterans. About half served in Germany or other areas in Europe. Many served in the United States. But about 25-30% were Vietnam veterans. Many had seen significant combat as well as atrocities committed by the Viet Cong and North Vietnamese. They had a stare in their eyes that was different than the other veterans. You could tell they were survivors. Many would not talk about their experiences mostly for the worry of being singled out as a killer of innocents. These men were impacted the most by the lack of respect for what they had endured. But while some of my friends were burning draft cards and discussing the best cities in Canada to go to for evading and escaping the draft, I was befriending these veterans. And many would open up to me and discuss their true feelings on what they had endured. Many were actually against the war. They knew that Ho Chi Minh, the leader of North Vietnam, was once our ally. We all wondered why we were supporting a corrupt South Vietnam regime. But in the end the discussion always centered on stopping communism and protecting the freedoms that we cherished for ourselves and the people of South Vietnam. I discovered that I was in the middle, as many Americans were. I was not sure what to think about the Vietnam War. I had grown up on John Wayne and Audie Murphy movies and anti-communist rhetoric. How did we stand up for the freedoms we cherished if not in Vietnam? After all, there was the "domino effect" of countries falling to communism. I was in a quandary.

May 1970 Academic Probation

Between college and work at the airport I had little time for anything else. I was still dating Diane but just barely. Her parents were now in the throes of separation that was leading to divorce. Her mother, a staunch Democrat and precinct worker was drunk constantly. She had been wailing since Nixon, a Republican, had won the election for president. And her marriage was falling apart. Somehow I think they blamed me for some of this turmoil. They refused to let Diane see me. She was grounded and having no car, no phone, and still in high school, no way really to see me. We drifted apart. At college I was doing no better. My grades the first semester were terrible. Spending all my time in the student union meant more time playing cards and talking to other students than working on my studies, and it showed. By

May of 1970 as I ended my first year of college my grade point average was 1.9 (in letter grade terms this would be a D grade). I was sent a letter advising me that I was on academic probation and that the following semester if I did not get my grades above 2.0 that the probation would continue. It also meant that I was now NOT in a draft deferment status and was subject to review by the draft board. I was at a crossroads. Also in May I met a beautiful young girl named Linda Van Hurst. Not able to see Diane for many months, this new girl stole my heart.

May 1970 Kent State Shooting and More War Protests

In April 1970 my brother Mike joined the Air Force to become an SP or Security Police. He did not plan on attending college and rather that getting drafted he decided to get a job he thought he would excel at. He also thought the Air Force would be safer and he had less of a chance of being sent to Vietnam. On May 4th 1970 the Governor of Ohio sent the National Guard to quell anti-war protests on the campus of Kent State University. Protests around the country were getting more violent and the Governor wanted to protect the university. Unfortunately the Guard had live ammunition and when the students became unruly the Guard fired on the crowd, killing four students and wounded nine others. These shootings led to further divisions around the country. We were a nation now deeply divided by the Vietnam War. Protests ignited around the country. The rock group Crosby, Stills, Nash & Young came out with the song "Ohio". In Vietnam the United States was now invading neighboring Cambodia and sending another 150,000 troops to the war zone. There were now 500,000 troops in the combat zone in Vietnam. Few families were untouched. Protests were so bad that 500 colleges in the United States were temporarily shut down.

Chapter Six:

Draft Number 144

As my latest Sunday afternoon was free I drifted off to sleep on the couch. It was a rare day when most of my family was gone from the house and all was very quiet. Having been up most of the night working the late shift I quickly fell sound asleep. I soon found myself in a very vivid and surreal dream. I was flying. It seemed effortless and I would fly down into forested valleys and along ridgetops. I was in total control and felt a sense of freedom that I had never felt before. It was as if I had wings and could fly anywhere with ease. Dreams are usually lost quickly after waking. But this dream would linger and I still remember it to this day.

The Nixon administration had decided to put a lottery system in place along with the draft so men of draft age would know their chances of being drafted. They would write one of 365 days on purple ping pong type balls and pull each one out individually. My birthday, February 2nd, was pulled on the 144th ping pong ball. So my draft number was 144. This meant I was in the 50% of the draft population that was highly likely. At least I wasn't in the top 10.

In the mean time I worked, would meet Linda from time to time, and very rarely would see Diane. I had no way of communicating with Diane as her mother was still screening all the phone calls and letters were useless. I gave up even trying. So occasionally she would just show up, stay for an hour, and quickly get back home.

July 25th

One afternoon in late July, around the 25th or so, Linda stopped by to say hello.

She said, "I have something important to talk to you about in private."

I said, "Sure come on in," and we went to my room for some privacy.

Not sure exactly what she wanted to discuss, I was off mentally thinking this was a "we need to go steady or break off the relationship" type of discussion.

As soon as I sat down Linda looked me in the eyes and said, "I'm pregnant."

You could hear my jaw hit the floor.

"Holy shit," I said.

And she nodded her head.

"I'm not sure what to do here," she said.

"Neither do I," I said.

We chatted for a little bit and decided that we needed to think about our options. I was in shock.

Chapter Seven:
What's Next?

July 26th

My mom grabbed me by the arm when I got home from work. It was the day after I talked to Linda and it was late. My mom usually was asleep by now but it was 11:30pm and she was still up. "You got a letter from the Government today; I think you should open it immediately."

She handed me the letter and a knife to open it. The letter was a week or 10 days old as it had been sent to our old address in Hazelwood and had been forwarded to our current home. It read:

"Greetings from the President: You are hereby ordered to report for induction into the Armed Forces......"

It was a draft notice and it had my name on it.

"Report on August 5th, 1970 to the Federal building room 303...."

I looked at my mom and handed her the letter.

"I thought that's what it was and I wanted you to see it right away," she said.

My response was, "Holy crap, what's next?"

July 28th

For the next few days I worked and worried about what my next steps would be. What do I do about Linda? I certainly needed to advise my employer that I was drafted and would likely not be working for them in a week or two, so I told them immediately. I also called Linda and told her that I received my draft notice and that we should meet in the next few days. It was my first day off in a couple of weeks and I wanted to meet later that day or the next. She advised me that tomorrow was best. So I had another day to ponder and worry about our predicament.

Then the phone rang. My mom said that it was Diane and she was calling from a pay phone.

"Hi Jim, I have a few hours that my parents didn't know about and I drove down to see you. We haven't seen each other in a while and I have something I want to talk with you about. I'm down the street at the Pizza Hut. Can you come and meet me?"

"Of course, give me a few minutes and I will be right there" was my response.

All I could think of was "Holy moly, how do I tell her about Linda?" Our meetings were very sporadic and we had not seen each other for four or five weeks. Frankly, I thought our relationship was done due to her parents' insistence that I not be involved with her. At the Pizza Hut we sat at a far corner table and ordered Cokes. The restaurant was empty except for the wait staff and cooks. It was good to see her again, but all I could think about was how would I tell her about Linda.

"Jim," she said, "I have something important to say so I'm just going to say it. I'm pregnant..."

I didn't say anything for maybe 30 seconds. I just blinked my eyes with shock. "Oh dear God," I thought, "what have I done?". My hands were shaking as Diane reached across the table and took my hand.

She said, "Don't worry, we'll figure it out."

But all I could think about was "How do I tell each of these girls… and what do I do?" I told Diane that I had just received my draft notice and I was to report for induction next week.

"Oh, that's why your hands were shaking. You have a lot going on in your life."

"Yes," I said, "a lot indeed!".

We chatted for perhaps another 30 minutes then she had to get home before her parents got suspicious. With no way of calling her I promised to write if we did not see each other before I left.

"We'll work it out," I said, "I know we will."

What Do I Do?

After my meeting with Diane I drove to a friend's house in Manchester. Dave was an Army veteran that I had met at Meramec College and he was always helpful with advice. He was 25 years old and had spent four years in the Army; three of those years in Heidelberg, Germany. He was cleaning one of his guns and invited me in to chat. He offered me a beer which I gladly accepted. "Dave," I said, "I've got a very good friend that needs some advice and I wonder if you would hear his story and let me pass on the advice?"

"Sure Jim, glad to help," he said.

I told him the story of this "fictitious" guy (me) and his pregnant predicament. I did not mention the draft notice until later because I did not want to spill the beans that it was my predicament.

"Hmmm," he mumbled, "that friend of yours is in a real pickle. I'd say he was fucked!" He got kind of a shit eating grin on his face and then said, "That's a no win situation. Your friend has just got to do the right thing".

He could probably see the weird look on my face so I spoke up and said, "Thanks Dave, I will pass that sage advice along to him. I think you're right, he's fucked. By the way, I got my draft notice yesterday. I will be the property of Uncle Sam by the end of next week."

"Oh you sorry sucker!" he said, "This calls for another beer!

So he pulled another German beer out of the cooler. Then another beer, and another, and another. Then he pulled out the hard liquor and poured some shots.

"This is how we drank in Germany" he said, and with that he poured a shot of cognac and dropped the full shot in his stein of beer and drank it down.

I woke up the next day in my bed at home not knowing how I got there. Dave had kindly called and paid for my cab ride home. It was six months prior to my 21st birthday. Hung over, I drank a glass of dill pickle juice with three aspirin. It was my grandmother's cure for hangovers. My mom was kind enough to give me a ride to Dave's house about a mile away. I knocked on Dave's door to get my car and he opened immediately with my car keys.

"You can really hold your liquor for a young guy," he said.

“Pickle juice” I said.

We both laughed. Then he winked at me and said, “Tell your FRIEND that I wish him luck.”

I forced a half smile on my face and got in my car and drove home. That brought me back to reality.

CHAPTER EIGHT:

THE RIGHT THING

Back at home my mom was worried about me.

"Why did you get so drunk last night?" she said.

I swallowed hard. "Mom, it's more than just the draft notice. Diane's pregnant."

And before I could say anything else she said, "Oh I really like Diane. Do you think you'll get married?"

"Well mom, there's more to it that that… Linda is pregnant too."

"Oh holy cow," she said, "What are you going to do?"

"I don't know mom, I'm still in shock from having two girls tell me they're pregnant and getting a draft notice in the space of four days." Then I said, "If dad was here and you and he were giving me advice together what would you recommend?"

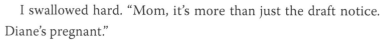

Mom just stared at me for the longest time. I could almost read the look on her face to say "the acorn doesn't fall far from the tree". But instead she said, "this is a predicament". "Jim you need to do THE RIGHT THING".

"Ok" I said, "What is the right thing?".

She turned away and walked over to the window and stared out and said, "You'll know".

But I did not know.

Army Vietnam Basic Training - Fort Polk, Louisiana

The next week flew by. I did not see Diane but I saw Linda twice. We had not come to any conclusion on what to do so we left it that we would stay in touch as best as possible. I arrived at the induction station in downtown St. Louis before 7am on August 5th.

Everyone got a physical. A few guys did not pass the physical and were classified as 4F. Boy were they happy!

Then the sergeant lined us up and said, "Count off in threes"

"One!"

"Two!"

"Three!"

"One!"

"Two!"

"Three!" was the shout down the lines of men.

"Alright, all the 'Threes' step forward. You, gentlemen, are now in the United States Marine Corps. The rest of you are United States Army."

And with that we were dispatched for testing and a bus ride to Fort Polk, Louisiana.

Chapter Nine:

Uncle Sam Needs Me - Basic Training at Fort Polk, LA

The first few weeks of basic were a blur. Marching, waiting in line, marching, waiting in line. All of our hair was shaved to the scalp. Boots and clothing, and everything else we would need to be a mean, green, fighting machine was issued. And we ran and marched everywhere.

We also took many tests. The army gave tests to determine the proper MOS (Military Occupational Specialty). After a particularly lengthy battery of tests were completed myself and three others were called into a room with a sergeant.

He said, "Troops, you have all four tested very high and it's customary for us to tell you that you can have your pick of MOS".

The guy next to me said, "Anything?"

"Within reason," the sarge said.

"How about helicopter flight school?"

"You bet," said the sergeant, "They need pilots."

"I'm in for that one sergeant," I said, as the other two said the same thing.

And in an instant I was targeted to a helicopter pilot MOS.

The funny thing was, I guessed on a lot of the questions. I must have guessed right. But this was only the first step. We needed to take a test called the FAST test which stood for Flight Actuation Simulation Test, as well as get a flight physical. These would take place in the next two weeks.

In my basic training unit there were about 200 troops made up of four platoons with about 100 guys or so to a floor. The building was an old un-air-conditioned WWII barracks. It had showers and toilets on one end where the drill sergeant's room was and double stacked bunk beds lining each side of the barracks. And it was hot. Louisiana in August and September is hot and humid.

It turns out that about half of the troops were drafted and the other half joined. There were many that joined specifically for warrant officer flight training; maybe 20 guys or so. It was one of the few officer positions in the military that did not require a college education so it was a pathway to fly helicopters and become an officer in the Army.

FAST Test - I'm Going to Flight School

The next few weeks we trained in military discipline, long marches, constantly exercised, and felt the wrath of our drill sergeant. Our day started at 4:30am. By 5am we were exercising; breakfast at 6am. Then training or testing until dinner.

During this time, myself and many of the other troops that had joined for WOC school (Warrant Officer Candidate school) were ushered to a facility to take the FAST test. Having worked at an airport and seen the inside of many cockpits, including a State Patrol Bell Helicopter, I had no problem with the questions on this test. But many did. Several guys flunked the test. These guys were out and sent to other MOS areas. But I had passed the test and was one step closer to getting into flight school.

After the FAST test we were scheduled for a flight physical. It was a basic physical but the toughest part was the eye exam and peripheral eye exam. They wanted pilots that could see 20/20 and sideways. Many more troops that had joined specifically for WOC school failed this portion. A lot of them were livid that they would not be moving forward to flight school. In fact, many just disappeared from our unit. I'm not sure if they had a contract broken and were able to get out of the Army or simply transferred to another training unit. But myself and the three other guys that tested into the program were all still on the list. But we still had to get through and graduate from Basic Infantry training.

You Can Really Light a Fart!

Basic training lasted about 10 weeks. During that time we learned a lot about combat fighting, weapons, and really began to gel as a fighting unit. We also started to kid around more as the men became comfortable in their barracks environment. The barracks were pretty sparse. The bathrooms had no stalls around the toilets so you just did your biological duty right there in front of the other guys.

This was difficult for some guys at first, but eventually we all became comfortable enough to take a crap in the open. Six or eight guys lined up in a row all taking a crap. Some guys were the constant butt of jokes as every crapper is unique. One day sitting in a line of crappers, the discussion erupted about whether it was possible to light a fart. Several guys from Louisiana were sure it was possible - they knew a lot about methane gas and they said that's all a fart was.

That night, after lights out at about 10pm, one of the Louisiana boys whispered loud enough for us to hear, "Check this out boys, if my butt blows up tell my mom I did it for science!"

And with that he lifted both knees up to his ears, held a Bic lighter down by the anal end of his white boxer shorts, lit the lighter and let 'er rip.

The blue flame shot out about twelve inches. And after a brief moment while we waited for his ass to explode (which did not happen) an enormous laugh rose up from the group. Of course this commotion woke the drill sergeant up from his room and he came charging out like a mad hornet.

"What the fuck is going on ladies?! Everybody out of bed and stand at attention!"

He queried the group to find out what happened but no one fessed up.

"Everybody down for 50 ladies!"

So all of us got down in a prone position and started doing pushups. The drill sergeant was still asking what had happened and was not going to stop until we came clean.

Finally, after our third set of 50 pushups, the Louisiana boy that lit the fart said, "Sergeant, I know what happened. I lit a fart sergeant and everybody erupted in laughter causing the unwanted commotion".

"You did what?"

"I lit a fart sergeant and it was a big one."

"All right ladies, UP OFF THE FLOOR and get to attention."

The drill sergeant got right in the face of Louisiana and said, "Do you realize that you could have blown your ass up?! And do you also realize that your ass is United States Government property?! And do you also realize that you could be court martialled for destroying United States Government property?!?! Back to bed boys, we're getting up an hour earlier tomorrow as we've got to work that gas out of you."

Though we had a grueling few days of cadence and exercise there was always someone in the barrack that would light a fart after lights out, including me. It became our way of shunning authority. We were a team.

Training for Vietnam

Vietnam was on everyone's mind. Even though he was elected on the political platform of getting the United States out of the Vietnam War, President Nixon was still sending troops to Vietnam. Many of the men in our unit expected orders to go there. So we took keen interest in all the combat training just in case our number was up and we received orders for 'Nam'.

It was now almost 10 weeks since I had been inducted. I had written both Linda and Diane. Linda sent letters back but I received nothing from Diane. I assumed her mom had intercepted them and she never saw them. But I kept sending them anyway just in case she would see one and see my return address to write. I told neither about the other and this was a burden on my soul.

I graduated from basic training in October. My mom actually drove to Louisiana for the graduation and without telling me, she brought Diane with her. It was great to see them both but due to scheduling of buses to flight school I only had about 20 minutes to talk to them.

Soon, I was on one of three buses driving to Mineral Wells, Texas where Fort Walters and the Army Basic Helicopter and Warrant Officer Training was located. There were guys from many different units going to flight school. Some had waited several weeks for the trip to Texas; others like me graduated and stepped right on the bus. It seemed like there was 150 or so of us.

CHAPTER TEN: IT STARTS WHEN YOU GET OFF THE BUS

Pre-Flight

The buses were loaded with some very anxious warrant officer candidates. Most of us knew nothing of what to expect once we arrived at Fort Walters. Many speculated that it could not be any worse than basic training in the heat of late summer Louisiana. But I held my tongue as I had spoken to a soldier that had failed and returned to Ft Polk for other duties. He advised me to be prepared for a tough five months of training. And he personally did not make it past the first month of Pre-Flight.

It was late October and the driver said we were in for a seven hour trip with one stop in Dallas. So we settled in for the ride and continued small talk speculation about the upcoming training and the war in Vietnam.

We arrived in the late afternoon and all three buses pulled up next to a nice white three story cinderblock building. There appeared to be a welcome committee waiting for us. It was made up of TAC officers that were Chief Warrant Officer 2 (CW2) and 1st Lieutenants. Think of them as drill sergeants on steroids, only worse. They wore white helmets and as soon as the buses stopped they started screaming for us to, "Get off the fucking bus and get in formation." We all did with great haste. Then they had us pour the contents of our duffle bags, basically ALL our worldly possessions, on the ground and proceeded to "knit pick" their way through anything they did not like. It was clear to me that this harassment was just the beginning.

A WO1 was eyeing me and he walked over and said, "What's your name candidate?"

"Sir, my name is Candidate James Crigler, sir!"

"You sound like you're from up north candidate Crigler and I don't like northerners. Where are you from Candidate?" he yelled.

"Sir, Candidate Crigler, I'm from Jackson Missouri which is right on the Mason Dixon line, sir."

"So, you are on the Mason Dixon Line. Well that is neither north or south Candidate Crigler and I require that all my candidates STAND FOR SOMETHING! What do you stand for Candidate Crigler?"

"Sir, Candidate Crigler, I stand for the rights and freedoms of the American people and I made a pledge to them in writing, up to and including my life, sir".

He seemed satisfied with my answer.

And so it continued for at least an hour with 8 or so TAC officers each harassing 10 or 20 men individually. Finally, after making us throw away most of what we had accumulated other than military garb, they made us re-pack our duffle bags and marched us into the building. We were paired up on one of three floors in the barracks. First floor was first flight, second floor was second flight, etc. We were randomly assigned to rooms holding three men each and told to pick a bunk, unpack and that we had 30 minutes before formation to march to dinner.

I Learn to Eat at Attention

Thirty minutes later we marched together as first flight to the WOC mess hall about 50 yards from the barracks. At dinner the harassment only increased. The TAC officers hovered all around us to make sure that WOC eating standards were up to their expectations.

We were required to stand at a table until all four chairs were occupied. Then we had to sit in unison and sit at attention. We all had to eat at the same time. No chatter, no talking, just chewing. And you BETTER have a cloth napkin in your lap! Once one WOC was finished he waited for the rest at sitting attention. Once we all were finished we stood up in unison, took our plates to the wash area, dropped them off and marched in fours back to our barracks.

This required much discipline from me. Having grown up in a very large family I was used to just shoveling the food in as soon as it hit my plate. I was learning the eating manners of an officer.

Formation at 2:00am

A TAC officer came through and advised us to be prepared for inspection in the morning. It was 10:00pm and lights out came shortly thereafter. In my room there were three very tired and stressed out warrant officer candidates.

My two new room mates were snoring way before I fell asleep. I stayed awake for a while thinking about the day to come. It seemed like no sooner had I closed my eyes when suddenly all hell broke loose. The TAC officers were running up and down the hallway making all kinds of racket.

"Get your asses up and get out in formation Candidates!"

" Get up, get up, get up and out to formation!"

It was 2:00am. The TAC officer that said we would be inspected in the morning was right. It WAS morning.

We all dressed as fast as we could but most of us were missing a boot or shirt or something. And the TAC officers ate us up. Up and down the line they went, taking apart everyone that was not perfectly dressed, which was all of us. I heard men sobbing in that line that night and also some grumbling.

At 3:00am we were released from formation and as we went back to our barracks rooms we all walked into rooms that had been torn apart. Everything was dumped on the floor and the beds were ripped apart as well. None of us slept the rest of the night. The next day there were two or three fewer warrant officer candidates.

Harass, Harass, Harass

Day two was much of the same. We ate breakfast sitting at attention and then marched off to a briefing room where all three flights were advised as to the schedule and rigors of the training.

"You will go to class daily for the first 30 days. We will have physical training daily. You will have quiet time for homework for your classes nightly from 7:00pm until 9:00pm. There will be

NO passes during the first month of Pre-flight," the TAC officer said. "After that, if you make it through Pre-Flight, classes will be half days and you will fly the other half."

And at that there was some applause in the room which the TAC officer quickly stopped.

"Candidates!" he said, "My job is to make sure that you have what it takes to be an Army aviator, A WARRANT OFFICER! And if you think this will be easy think again!

"I want you to look at me! Now look at the man on your right. Now look at the man on your left. Now look back at me. The two people you just looked at besides me WON'T BE HERE!"

And that TAC officer was right. The courses and studies were intense. We studied weather, map reading, aerodynamics of flight, mathematics, military protocol. We learned all the instruments we would use and how they worked in flight. We learned about each of the different types of helicopters that we would train in at Fort Walters. We even studied English composition, my worst ever subject.

And we were tested daily. If you got less than 70% on a test you had to retake it. If you did not get at least 80% on the retake you failed and were kicked out of the program. This was a lot of pressure for most guys that did not go to college. And it showed. Between the harassment of the TAC officers for even the most minor infraction and the difficulty of the studies, many men either failed or gave up.

Several times I came back to the barracks to find that my room mates were now brand new. Their roommates had failed or quit and we were consolidated.

Pray Like Hell

I was doing pretty well in all of the initial courses but continued to get super harassed by several of the TAC officers. Occasionally, they would size a WOC up and see if he was good enough to handle the stress. But it felt like they were just out to get you. They were relentless on me. As our rooms were inspected daily by the TAC officers when we were at class I would regularly return to my room and find all of MY drawers dumped on the floor, but my two roommates' drawers untouched. This along with the normal extraordinary harassment pushed me to the edge. But something inside of me refused to give up.

Since my bout with the uncontrolled teenage erection at the seminary I had gradually moved away from the Church. It seemed way too controlling and had too much pomp and ceremony for me. I just thought that God had to be easier to talk to than all that ceremony. But now I needed some help from up above. I decided to attend the service on base given for the WOCs. I did not care what denomination it was, I just wanted to be there. Never in my life have I prayed so hard for the courage and stamina to withstand this training. I was there well after everyone left.

As I was walking out of the service one of the Super Seniors (a warrant officer candidate that had graduated from Fort Walters and was awaiting a class assignment at the next phase of flight training in Fort Rucker, Alabama) that was at the service struck up a conversation with me.

"How's it going candidate?" he said, "You looked like you were praying pretty hard back there in the service. Episcopalians usually don't pray that hard."

"I'm not Episcopalian," I said, "I grew up Catholic but now you could call me just a Christian. But I guess I was praying for strength pretty fervently back there."

He asked if I was in Pre-flight and I said, "Yes, and they are really giving it to me!"

"Look," he said, "let me give you some advice. Your TAC officer's job is to see if you will break under pressure. If you break here in training you will surely fail in combat. Show them you will never give up and fix every minor issue they find. Pay attention Candidate. Eventually they will be satisfied."

I thanked him and walked back to the barrack. I would take his advice and discovered he was absolutely right.

The Discipline of Hard Study

The discipline of study was good for me. Unlike the casual study time at the student union at Meramec College, this was forced quiet time of two hours nightly. And it taught me to concentrate and learn. The Army taught through a method called "Programed Learning." You would listen to the instructor, study and read in the evening. Then take a pre-test to assess your understanding. Then take the main test in class.

We were allowed to smoke in our rooms, which I did. And only occasionally was I distracted by my roommate WOC Larry Oakley when he spit his Skoal tobacco dip into his coke bottle. It didn't bother me until he filled it right up to the top of the bottle. As he continued to spit it was hard not to watch when it might spill over the edge. It never did.

Chapter Eleven:
I Can Fly!

Flight Line After 30 days of Hell

Finally, in what seemed more like six months instead of one, our first month of pre-flight was over. We had lost many men from our unit. Just like the Super Senior had advised me, the TAC officers continued to see who would break under pressure, and many men did. But so far I had made it.

Now we would begin the next four months with half days of classroom training and half days of flying. The big discussion of all the WOCs in my flight was regarding what it would be like to finally get into the air.

There was somewhat less harassment than the first four weeks but we were still held to a very high standard of discipline. Occasionally you would still hear a TAC officer dressing down one of the WOCs but this was nowhere near the level of harassment that we received before. We were also now VERY spit and polished. To survive the first month EVERYTHING had to be in order to pass daily inspections. We were all extremely well organized. Never having been held to a clean room growing up, this experience had changed me. For the rest of my life I would be organized because of this training.

Solo and Hovering

It was now late November 1970. The WOC flights rotated classroom time, mornings or afternoons depending on helicopter and instructor pilot availability. But being on the flight line was thrilling. It was also stressful. We were told that we could not solo prior to 10 hours of flight time but we were required to solo by 20 hours of flight time. If we could not get the hang of it by then we'd get another couple flight hours with a different instructor pilot. If you could not solo by then you failed and would be out of the WOC program.

Training started in a little two seater Hughes TH55. These small helicopters looked like little bumble bees and sounded like them too. Occasionally we flew a somewhat larger helicopter called a Hiller OH-23. But most of my time was in a TH55. The instructor pilot, also known as the IP, would take us up in the air, find an area where there was relatively little air traffic (hard to do when there were over a hundred helicopters flying at once), then give us the controls and let us get the feel of the helicopter.

No sooner had we got comfortable on this first flight with "straight and level" flying when the IP would cut power by twisting the power control on the collective. This would happen on our first flight and every subsequent flight.

"What are you going to do? A bullet just shot your engine out," he would say. "Lower collective... where are you going to land? Get your airspeed up!"

And so it went. Our training to land without power began from the first hour of flight training.

Straight and level flight was not difficult. So the IP would add lots of things for you to think about.

"Where is your reference point so you can return to the base? Keep us at a steady altitude! Where will you land if the engine cuts out? Always be looking for a landing area!" he would constantly say as you were flying and trying to get comfortable.

But the toughest thing to master for many WOCs was the task of hovering. We would fly out to a rather secluded field area, usually four or five acres square, and commence learning to hover. At first I was all over that field. But gradually I got the feeling of control and confidence to fly at a hover on that small cushion of air below the aircraft. In spite of the rather cool temperatures of late fall, we would return from these sessions with our Nomex flight suits soaked in sweat. You could not solo until you mastered the art of hovering.

You never knew when the IP was going to let you solo. When it was my turn, we were practicing autorotations at the main air field asphalt runway. This involves cutting the engine power and lowering the collective which causes the main rotor blades to reduce pitch and then eventually go to a negative pitch setting. The force of the wind flowing upward through the blades from the helicopter falling causes the main rotor blades to continue to spin and provide control. As you approached ten to 20 feet above the runway at 50-60 knots you flared, which slowed your forward speed and then used the inertia of the spinning main rotor blades to cushion your landing by applying lift via the collective.

My IP just looked at me after one of these landings and said, "You have the aircraft."

He unbuckled his seatbelt and stood outside the bird.

Before he unplugged his helmet he said, "Do three take offs and flight patterns around the field and land to a hover. On the third one land to the ground and I will come back out. I need a cigarette and a coffee. Now get your solo out of the way!"

With that he unplugged his mic and shut the door.

There is this sudden awkward moment where you feel a little panic. But you take a deep breath, slowly come to a hover, call the tower for takeoff. Then you inch the cyclic forward to increase air speed until you slowly attain transitional lift. Flying straight for a couple hundred yards you make a climbing turn left then come level at 500 feet, then level downwind to a couple hundred yards past the runway, then left turn back towards the runway for your final approach as you call the tower for landing.

After my second landing to a hover and takeoff I was feeling pretty confident. By the time I landed and the IP got into the bird I was exuberant. I had soloed!

The IP smiled a big grin and said, "Pretty good flying candidate."

When we shut down and debriefed for the day the IP handed me the customary "Hover Bug Card" which each IP would fill out, sign, and date. We cherished our Hover Bug Cards. Mine was dated December 17th, 1970. I still have the signed Hover Bug Card to this day.

On the bus ride back to the barracks it was also customary to stop at the Holiday Inn in Mineral Wells and march all the candidates that soloed that day to the swimming pool. There, four WOCs would grab you by a limb and launch you, flight suit and all, into the pool. Getting out of the pool you would walk ceremoniously under the two crossed Huey blades that were near the pool. The sign on the blades said "Through these blades pass the finest pilots in the world." I was feeling pretty good.

CHAPTER TWELVE:

WHY DOES A PILOT NEED TO LEARN ENGLISH COMPOSITION?

It was around this time that our instructions included my least favorite subject, English composition and writing skills. I just could not figure out why we needed this instruction to fly. So I copped my typical "Don't like English" attitude, studied very poorly, and promptly failed the test. I also failed the re-test. Suddenly, I was in a situation where I could be kicked out of flight school. My instructor told me that at this stage of training I would be given another test, much tougher, and if I failed it I was out of WOC training. I had two days to study and was then to report to a separate testing area.

It was February 4th, 1971, two days after my 21st birthday. We had a little over one month left in our first phase of primary flight training before we shipped off to Fort Rucker, Alabama for advanced instrument flight training and Huey flight training. I was kicking myself for not taking serious interest in my English studies. My contact with Linda and Diane was sporadic. I'm sure their lives were hectic but mine was extremely busy. There was very little time to write.

A Child is Born

On February 6th I was called and advised to report to the commanding officer's office. I had never been called there before and was sure this had something to do with my failing the English tests. The commander's office was intimidating. At the entrance there were two yellow feet painted on the floor where you had to put your feet as you requested permission to enter. On the right side of the door at about shoulder level was a yellow square where you were to knock three times and announce yourself.

"Sir, Candidate Crigler reporting as ordered, sir!"

The captain looked up at me and said, "Yes, come in Candidate Crigler."

I marched to the front of his desk and stopped where two additional yellow feet were painted on the floor in front of the desk. I stopped, came to attention, and saluted.

He let me hold my salute for about 10 seconds before he saluted back and said "At ease Candidate."

I put my hands behind my back, spread my feet somewhat and took the "at ease" stance.

"Candidate Crigler, I was not aware that you were married," he said.

"Sir, Candidate Crigler, I am NOT married, sir."

"Well Candidate Crigler, I have before me a telegram from the Red Cross that is advising you that you are the father of a 7 pound 10 ounce baby girl born this morning by a Linda Van Hurst. Is this a joke Candidate Crigler?"

"Sir, Candidate Crigler, this is no joke, sir."

"You mean you actually fathered this child candidate?"

"Sir, yes, sir. I plan on doing the right thing, sir."

The captain stared down at the telegram again and then set it over to the side of his desk. He laid it on top of the Bible he kept there.

He said, "Candidate Crigler, do you realize that an officer in the United States Army has to have a certain moral code?"

"Sir, Candidate Crigler, YES SIR," I said.

"Well Candidate Crigler, are you sure that you have the morals to become an officer in the United States Army and that this incident will not bring disgrace to our corps?"

"Sir, Candidate Crigler, I'm certain that I have the morals to be one of the best officers in the Army sir. I will do the right thing, so help me God," I said.

He looked up at me for about 30 seconds and then he said, "Congratulations Candidate. You are dismissed."

And with that I came to attention, saluted, turned, and vacated the office. I was soaked in sweat. What the hell was I going to do? And what was the right thing?

English Re-Test and a Lucky Break

I had studied my butt off at every opportunity during those two days. Then I reported to the testing site for those trainees that did the unthinkable, failing a test twice (after soloing). Upon reporting to the room for the test a captain greeted me. I was the ONLY ONE to be tested that day and the pressure was on. He advised me that I had one hour to complete the test and that when I was finished to see him for grading. He said I needed at least an 80 percent to pass and stay in the WOC course.

He knew there was a lot of pressure on me to pass this test so he said, "Just relax and take the test."

This test was hard for me but I finished in the allotted time. I handed the test to the captain and waited outside of his office while he graded the paper. Much of this test was subjective.

After I sweated bullets for about 10 minutes he called me back into his office. My test was sitting on top of his desk. I could clearly see the number 79 circled on the front page. My heart sank.

The captain looked at me and said, "Where you from Candidate?"

"I lived around the St. Louis area sir," I said.

"Well what part of St. Louis?"

"Well sir, my family lived all over St. Louis as we moved quite often. But my favorite place to live was in Kirkwood, Missouri."

"Really?" he said, "I'm from Kirkwood too, where did you live?"

"Sir, I lived at 109 Geyer Road."

"No way," he said, "That was a Carmelite nuns convent. I used to do work on the grounds at that place."

"Yes sir, you are right. But in 1962 the convent was vacant and my family, who was struggling at the time, received the generosity of St Peter's Parish and allowed us to live there until my dad got back on his feet. I lived there for 18 months and also went to St Peter's Catholic school and was an altar boy as well."

"You're right," he said, "I remember when it was vacated. There weren't a lot of Carmelite nuns left and they consolidated. I also went to St Peter's Parish."

As we chatted I could see him doodling on the top page of the test. I figured he was just being nice to me before he advised me that I was shipping out of WOC training. But instead he turned the test around, slid it towards me and said, "Candidate Crigler, get back to your training unit. You passed with an 82%."

My jaw dropped as I looked at the test. The 79 had turned into an 82. I had dodged a big bullet.

Chapter Thirteen: The Morals of an Officer

I Learn to be a Real Pilot

I fired off a letter to Linda and also got one in return announcing from her that my daughter was named Carrie. I'm not sure what happened to me but I suddenly became more disciplined and more focused. I had a reason to be good besides just getting my wings. The future would see the kind of person that I was.

In the mean time we continued classes and flying daily. I studied hard for every class and learned all the detail of flight. I wanted to be the best pilot in the Army.

On the flight line we continued to learn every aspect of flight. We were now soloing regularly and flying without the IP. We had various automobile tires that were painted different colors that we could practice remote landings to. White tires were safe to land for any candidate. Yellow could be landed to only with check off from an IP as they were more difficult. And red tires could only be landed at with an IP on board as they were pretty treacherous. So land we did, over and over and over until we got pretty good flying and landing those birds.

The IP would also fly with us daily. We had to ALWAYS be looking for a safe place to land in case of engine failure (or IP rolling the throttle off). You never knew when your IP would cut the engine and then judge you on how well you reacted and put the aircraft in a position for safe landing. Eventually it became second nature for us to do this. For many of us, this would be a lifesaver in Vietnam.

We would also do autorotations to the ground daily until it became a second nature way to land. There were also many other emergency situations that we trained for. Running landings to simulate a no hydraulics landing, tail rotor failure, and many others.

We were in our last month of primary flight training and the men still remaining in the company were now tough, disciplined, and getting to be very good pilots. Few men ever drop out or fail at this stage of the training. We were now considered seniors by the TAC officers. The harassment was the least it had been so far in the WOC training.

A Child is Born - Again

On February 25th I was flying with my IP and doing some of the best autorotations of my training. Suddenly the tower calls for Candidate Crigler to return to the airfield immediately. I flew the aircraft back to the tower area, gave my seat up to my flight buddy and walked over to the briefing room.

There waiting for me were 2 MP (Military Police) and a jeep.

"What's up?" I said, "Am I under arrest for something?"

The MP closest to me said, "No, you're not under arrest. Your company commander requested that we pick you up and return you from the flight line for an urgent meeting."

So we all hopped in the jeep and headed back to my barracks where the commander's office was.

I moved quickly towards the captain's office. Then, stepping precisely on the two yellow footprints in front of his door I came to attention and knocked three times on the yellow square on the right of his entrance.

"Sir, Candidate Crigler reporting as ordered, sir."

The captain was sitting at his desk and he looked very upset. His face was red and he almost looked as if he was weeping. I stood there for about 30 seconds before he replied.

"Yes, come in Candidate Crigler."

I marched straight ahead and planted my feet on the two yellow footprints in front of his desk, came to attention and saluted. I held the salute for a long time, maybe 30 seconds, maybe even a minute. The captain never saluted back. I finally drew down my salute and remained at attention.

Normally the officer would tell the candidate to stand "at ease" but I would remain at attention during this entire meeting. I could see two telegrams setting on the captain's desk. One was open and laid to his right near his Bible. The other telegram was closed and had a note written near it. LAM SON 719 the note read in bold letters.

The captain picked up his small Bible and started patting it in his left palm.

"Candidate Crigler, I have here before me a Red Cross telegram. It says that your daughter Lisa was born today and weighs 7 pounds 10 ounces and that the mother 'Diane' is doing fine. Candidate Crigler, is this a mistake?"

"Sir, Candidate Crigler, Diane is not a mistake, nor is my daughter. But I have made a big mistake in my life and I will make it right, sir."

"Well Candidate Crigler, did we not have a discussion on the type of morals that are required to be an officer in the United States Army?"

"Sir, YES SIR. Sir, this is not something I did on purpose or as an immoral act," I said.

"Shut the fuck up Candidate!" he said, as he stood up and walked around his desk.

Still patting the Bible in his left palm he got very close to my face and said, "Candidate, you do not have the morals of a jackass. Being a warrant officer pilot requires maintaining control and thinking on your feet, NOT thinking through the head of your PECKER! Your decisions in the future will either save or lose men's lives. Which head will you think through in Vietnam, Candidate Crigler?!"

"Sir, Candidate Crigler, the one on top of my shoulders, sir," I said.

"Candidate Crigler, I'm extremely disappointed in you. So much so that I would like you to resign from WOC training. There are men in Vietnam much better than you or me dying. They are men that graduated under my command and THEY ARE FUCKING DYING! And you are thinking through the head of your dick!"

"Sir, I will not resign. I know this looks bad. But this situation is one that I can fix. It will not bring dishonor to the United States Army and I will do whatever is necessary to make it right, sir. I am now the father of two, not one. It is my responsibility as a father as well as a future officer to show a good example, sir, and to finish what I start. I will not resign, sir, because the Army would be losing one of its best future warrant officer pilots. Sir."

I'm not sure where those words came from. I just blurted them out. Perhaps they just came right from my heart.

The captain was silent for a moment, probably trying to figure out if I was trying to bullshit my way through this situation. He walked back to the other side of his desk and set the Bible down.

"Crigler, I'm going to be one tough son of a bitch on you but I'm not going to require that you resign today. You may want to resign tomorrow. But we'll see."

Then, he picked up the other telegram and in a broken voice he said, "There are men much braver than you and me dying right now. Get the fuck out of my office, Candidate."

I saluted, turned and marched out of there as fast as I could. I went directly to my barrack room to find my drawer dumped on the floor. This was not a good sign.

We had less than a month to graduate primary flight training and I was determined that nothing was going to make me resign. The captain kept his word and instructed the TAC officer on my flight to make life hell for me. Which he did! Several times I heard men talking about whether I would make it through the next week or not. They did not know what happened but they knew I was on someone's hit list.

I got all the extra duties in addition to my classes and flight time. My day started at 4:00am and ended at 11:00 or 11:30pm. I cleaned toilets with toothbrushes. I stood inspection while others got time off to go off base. I was awakened in the middle of the night to recite various Army standing orders, I had extra physical training. But I would not give up. I would not resign. Then, as quickly as the extra harassment started, it stopped. It was early March 1971.

LAM SON 719

Back on the flight line we continued to improve our skills. The instructor pilots were much less strict on us now and much friendlier. I had now been assigned to a warrant officer IP that had recently returned from Vietnam and he was one hell of a pilot.

One day after our flying we were in a debriefing session and I noticed on his note pad the words LAM SON 719. These were the same words written on the telegram that the Commander had on his desk.

So I asked him, "What does LAM SON 719 mean?"

He said, "It's a total fuck up of a mission. Nixon is experimenting using only ARVN (South Vietnamese troops) and NO United States ground troops on large missions, but they are supporting these attacks with U.S. Helicopter resources. This is so he can tell the American public that there are no U.S. troops on the ground in Laos. But he's not telling them they ARE in the AIR! Rumor has it that there are over 600 helicopters being used on this mission to Laos and Ho Chi Minh trail. It's called LAM SON 719.

"I got a letter from a buddy I used to fly with. He says over 400 aircraft were shot down. Many of my friends have died in that fucking mission."

So now I knew why the Commander was so upset. He too had lost a friend in LAM SON 719.

Chapter Fourteen: Mother Rucker

Instrument Training

We were jubilant on the last day of primary flight school at Fort Walters, Texas. We would not be officers and wear wings yet but we had conquered the toughest part of the Warrant Officer Flight Training. And we each had more flight time than most civilian helicopter pilots ever got. We were all hot shot pilots.

On March 26th, 1971 we graduated from primary flight school.

The Army gave us all orders to report to Fort Rucker, Alabama for advanced flight training. We had a little less than a week to get there. I drove north to St. Louis with a friend in my flight platoon, WOC Robert Strong.

I dropped Robert off at his home and spent a couple of days with my family, met with Linda and saw Carrie for the first time. I also tried to get in touch with Diane, but as usual her mom screened the calls. I still wonder how a person could drink so much and not keel over from liver failure? But at least I had tried.

A few days later I picked up Robert and we continued on to Fort Rucker.

Once we reached Rucker and our unit we were assigned to a barracks and settled in. Rucker was much more like a school instead of the officer-candidate harassment we had previously received. I can't ever remember being inspected but all of us kept the same standards of organization and discipline.

Most of the married guys in class lived off base in some of the many trailer parks around the area. But the schooling was just as intense as primary flight school. This phase of instruction started with instrument flight training. We had to learn how to fly the aircraft without visually looking outside.

In the aircraft this was accomplished wearing a hood of sorts on our helmet that gave us zero view to the sides. We could only look forward at the instrument panel. In classroom training we used what was called a 'link trainer' which was basically a sealed oblong box that moved to simulate flight (and give you the experience of vertigo without actually flying) with all the instruments of a Huey so you could practice.

The actual flying was done in a Bell TH-13. But both were very difficult to get used to. Most guys regularly came out soaking wet with sweat after an hour in the link trainer. But this training was necessary as Vietnam was prone to wet monsoons and sometimes foggy weather.

Huey Training

After approximately 40 hours of instrument hood time training we got our initiation to the UH-I or the Huey. The trainer aircraft were all Alpha or Bravo models, meaning UH-1A or UH-1B models. These were like flying Cadillacs compared to the aircraft that we were used to flying. They did not require all the throttle adjustments to engine speed. This was automatic so the main rotor blade revolutions per minute maintained 6600 RPM. This left valuable concentration time to do other flight activities like concentrating on actually flying the bird instead of cross-checking the RPM constantly. It was an amazing bird to fly.

The instructors took us through all of the same emergency procedures in the Huey that we practiced in the smaller aircraft. We practiced many, many autorotations along with tail rotor failures and, most important, the hydraulic failure running landings. You could fly these birds without hydraulics but you could not land to a hover and maintain control. With hydraulics failure you could only do a running landing.

For the next four months we would train in the Huey. It was much easier to learn and develop flight skills without the harassment and constant inspections of primary flight school. Perhaps this is what it was like to go through flight training as an officer.

Each WOC class was shadowed by an officer class made up of a few higher ranking officers but mostly 1st and 2nd Lieutenants who took the same training minus the Warrant Officer Candidate harassment. We were now treated more like students than Candidates. Even the weekends were easier. We all fondly started referring to our base of operations as 'Mother Rucker.'

Panama City, FL

After the first month of Rucker training we all realized that we actually had weekends off and did not have to cram our studies or prepare for inspections. So we would hop in our cars and head to the panhandle of Florida and a little town called Panama City. For guys growing up in the Midwest this was heaven.

I would regularly go with a fellow WOC I met from Chicago, Herb Koenig. Herb and I would drive down the two lane roads, often stopping at farm stands that sold boiled peanuts, and finish the two hour drive at the beach. We would grab a six pack of beer and sit on the beach eating our boiled peanuts, drinking beer and discussing all the 'what ifs' of our future as Army helicopter pilots. Vietnam was constantly on our minds and we were keen to keep up with the Paris peace talks.

Graduation - My Biggest Accomplishment

Finally, on August 24th 1971 the Warrant Officer Rotary Wing Class 71-25 graduated from flight school.

We had to first be sworn in as officers on August 23rd. We would now be addressed as "Mister" which was the military protocol for warrant officer names. I was now a WO1 or commonly referred to as a 'Wobbly 1.' It was the absolute biggest accomplishment of my life. I was now Mister Crigler! The ceremony included all the students in the Officer Class, foreign students from Germany and Vietnam, and all of the warrant officers like me. We were all jubilant, officers and warrants alike. We were now Army aviators.

CHAPTER FIFTEEN:

YOU ARE A WALKING DEAD MAN!

An Angry Father and Three Weeks Leave

Orders came out the next day. In my class 98 warrant officers graduated. 97 of us had assignments to Vietnam. We had about three weeks leave before we had to catch a flight to Vietnam and report to Tan Son Nhut air base in Saigon for our in-country assignment. The Army did not assign you to a unit in Vietnam until you got in-country as the need for pilots could change in each unit depending on the war situation.

The day after I graduated I purchased a brand new Corvette and drove it off the showroom floor. It was my gift to myself for the last year of hard work. It was midnight blue with a T-top. When I got back to my barracks and got out of the car a private first class was walking by.

He saluted and said, "Good day, sir!"

I hesitated and then quickly saluted back. It was the first time anyone had given me the respect of a salute.

I drove my new Corvette back to St. Louis the next day. My parents and my brothers and sisters were in the process of packing up. They would be moving to Chicago for my dad's new job a couple weeks after I left for Vietnam. But I just wanted to relax. I called Linda and told her about my orders and met with her several times.

I also called Diane. This time her mother let me talk to her. I advised her that I was home for a few weeks and if she had time I would like to see her. She said she would try.

War Protesters at a Fever Pitch

Vietnam War protests were everywhere. It was now early September 1971 and not only were there protests in Washington, D.C., people were protesting to the returning soldiers coming back from Vietnam. On the nightly news I saw people throwing eggs at buses carrying returning soldiers and shouting "baby killer." This was beyond the protests that I had seen in college before getting drafted. Parts of the country were now targeting the soldiers, especially in northern California where most soldiers passed through on their way back from Vietnam. The soldiers had no choice. The politicians did.

Draft Dodgers go to Toronto

Many of the friends I had made in college, other than the Veterans, were very against the war. While I was on leave I tried to look up some of these guys and they were nowhere to be found. Funny, their parents did not say, "They went to Canada to evade the draft." They just said, "He's on a trip up North."

I was shocked at how many men were avoiding their duty. But the country was extremely divided and I suppose they were taking a stand that they thought was right.

A Father Confronts Me

Three days before I was to depart for Vietnam I was sitting at home talking to one of my younger brothers about flying. It was about 10:00am when a car drove up and an older gentleman and Diane got out and knocked on the kitchen door. It was Diane's father Bob Pastors and he asked if he could come in and talk to me in person.

In the entire time I dated Diane I can't remember ever talking to Bob Pastors. In fact I had only seen him one or two times in all the years of dating. We invited them in and while my mom ushered my younger brothers and sisters into another room we all sat at the kitchen table. Bob was clearly pissed.

He said, "Jim you have caused our family great distress and I am extremely upset with you."

My mom chimed in, "it takes two people to do this Bob, not one."

Bob gave my mom a nasty glare and I thought for sure he was going to do something physical. But he just looked back at me and said, "What are you going to do about this situation Jim?"

Not knowing what to say I said, "I'm not sure, sir".

And at that moment I decided that I would tell Bob and Diane why I had hesitated and the REAL situation that I had to figure out.

"Bob, Diane, there is something that I need to tell you..."

But just then Bob shouted out in a burst of anger, "you don't need to tell us a thing!" Look Jim, do you realize that as a helicopter pilot your odds of surviving the war are zero?!" He was so angry he was spitting as he talked. "You are a walking dead man," he said. "The least you can do is marry Diane and give her your name so that when you are killed at least she will get the military insurance money to help raise Lisa."

My mind was reeling. Was this the real reason? Just the money? What about your daughter's feelings? He could have said, "Don't worry Jim, we will all get through this together and I will help in any way I can." But instead he used other words of anger.

I looked over at my mom and her face was ashen. She was so proud that I was now an officer and Army aviator that she had not thought about the consequences of war and the death of her eldest son. But Bob Pastors had put that issue right on the kitchen table for all of us to ponder.

I looked up at Bob and Diane and said, "I'm sorry, I can't."

Diane looked over at me and said, "I'm sorry Jim, I'm embarrassed and did not want my dad to come here."

And with that Bob Pastors got up, grabbed Diane by the arm and led her out to the car. "We're getting out of here. Jim, you will have to live with this decision."

No one at that table knew it but I had already decided on my $20,000.00 military insurance policy. I had split the beneficiary 50/50 between Diane and Linda the day I received the policy.

Chapter Sixteen:
A Leap of Faith

A Grandmother and Her Lucky Rosary

That same afternoon I got a call from my grandmother, Florence Feltmeier.

She said, "Jimmy, I was not able to wish my son Bill off during World War ll. As you know, he was killed on the beaches of Tarawa with most of his Marine unit. You are leaving for Vietnam in a couple of days and I would like to meet with you prior."

So we set a meeting for the next day at her house in University City, Missouri.

The next day I sat down with my grandmother.

She said, "Jimmy, I want to wish you much luck on the missions I fear you will be on in Vietnam. The news about the War is terrible and the crews that are flying in those helicopters are getting some of the worst of it.

"It was the same in WWII, except that the public was more behind the soldiers. We lost Bill in 1943 and I so wish I had been able to wish him off and give him some good luck and motherly advice. You have been like the son that I lost and I have something special for you. It's the rosary I always let you use when we would go to early mass at St. Rita's Church. I had the priest bless it especially for you," she said.

"I want you to keep it on you at all times when you are flying as I'm sure it will bring you good luck."

"Sure Grandma, I will keep it in my pants zipper pocket of my flight suit," I said.

"Good. There is one more thing, and this you have to promise me," she said. "The Lord's Prayer is very powerful. I want you to say it before EVERY take off and EVERY landing."

"I'll try Grandma," I said.

"No Jim, you have to PROMISE me that you will do this!"

"Ok Grandma, I promise," I said.

I would keep that promise to my grandmother. During the entire 12 months in Vietnam I always had that rosary in my right calf flight suit pocket. And every take off and every landing I said the Lord's Prayer (although due to the chaos of many combat missions this was sometimes abbreviated to just the words "our father"). To this very day, on every commercial jet flight that I take, during take offs and landings I quietly recite the Lord's Prayer in my mind.

CHAPTER SEVENTEEN: VIETNAM - A NEWBIE

The Plane Ride

We boarded the big Boeing 707 at Travis Airforce base in California. Every one of us was in khaki summer uniforms and 95% of us going to Vietnam for the first time. There must have been 200 soldiers on this flight. And I knew none of them. The seats were configured so that there were three seats on each aisle facing three other seats. So you had six soldiers to a row facing six other soldiers. We were packed in that plane like sardines and for the 18 hour flight it got quite uncomfortable.

In 1971 you were allowed to smoke cigarettes on aircraft. On this flight there was no non-smoking section. So we all smoked and tried to sleep as much as possible. I can't imagine what it was like for the guys that didn't smoke. It seemed like everyone was smoking a cigarette.

Many of the men were walking the aisles and standing in groups discussing what was about to happen in their lives. After five or six hours we made a brief stop in Hawaii to refuel. We were all restricted to a small area of the terminal. Those that could bought more cigarettes.

Finally, after what was the longest flight of my life, the captain came on the intercom and advised that we would be approaching Tan Son Nhut Air Base in Saigon in a few minutes and to buckle up. Two minutes after the announcement, the plane made a hard right, then a hard descending left turn, and what had to be the steepest approach I have ever been on to this day in any jetliner. Clearly that pilot wanted to get the jet on the ground and fast. In the passengers section no one said a word. We all knew we were now in a war zone.

This Place is Like an Oven

I was sitting in one of the first three rows so I was able to get off the plane pretty quickly. I remember the stewardess smiling and nodding her head as we passed and walked out the door to the metal stairs that were rolled up to the plane. It was like walking into an outside oven. It must have been 110 degrees. The air was so thick that your clothes were instantly wet with perspiration and humidity.

Curse words would flow freely as each man walked out the cabin door into the atmosphere. We were all herded over to a group of green buses with wire mesh over the windows (to prevent Vietcong from lobbing hand grenades into the transfer buses) and from there were bused to a receiving station where the officers were separated and we received temporary sleeping quarters.

The rooms were not air-conditioned but at least they had showers where you could cool off before hitting the bed. Sleep did not come easy on that first night. We were now on the opposite side of the world. For our bodies it was daytime.

Brush Your Teeth With Red Dye

The next day we had several stations that all new "in country" soldiers had to go through. The first was brushing your teeth with a red dye so that you could see all the plaque on your teeth. Apparently tooth decay was a major reason to lose a soldier from the battlefield.

Then we were given pamphlets on customs and etiquette in Vietnam. They also gave us a few words and various meanings. That afternoon I was in the flight assignment shack talking to a 2LT about unit assignments.

He said, "Well, it's pretty open so you can go anywhere in Vietnam that you choose."

"My brother Mike is in Phan Rang Air Base with the Airforce. Is there a unit close to Phan Rang?' I asked.

"Sure, the Cavalry has a unit on the edge of the air base right out there with Charlie. A Troop 7th of the 17th Air Cav. You want that assignment?" he said.

"Who is Charlie?" I said.

"Oh man, are you a fucking newbie! Viet Cong is also shortened to VC. The phonetic alphabet calls the letters V and C Victor Charlie. We just shorten it to Charlie."

"You mean the enemy attacks them regularly?" I said.

"It's been pretty quiet on the war front lately but understand this newbie, we could all be attacked anywhere, any time."

With that I gave him the thumbs up for A Troop 7/17 Cav. I would have orders in hand tomorrow.

Poker Game and Prostitutes

That evening after chow we had two new arrivals in our temporary sleeping quarters. There were eight officers that arrived with me. Two 1LT's and six WO1 pilots all right out of flight training. The two new arrivals were not coming in country, they were leaving. Both were Huey pilots and both were loud and obnoxious and drunk as hell. They were on the first flight out the next day going back to the "World" and they were determined to have one last bash. The captain was talking of one last fling with the prostitutes and ushered the CW2 that was with him out the door.

We were frankly pretty glad those guys left. But in a few minutes they were back, apparently blocked by the MPs and told they had to stay on base. But now they wanted a card game and pulled out some cards and military script money (the Army would take away all the US greenback dollars and replace them with military script which we used for purchases) and the chief warrant officer hollers, "Ok you newbie fucks, who's in the game?"

Myself and one of the 1LTs stepped forward and the four of us proceeded to play poker. Now I don't believe I am a good poker player, but that night either luck was with me or the two good players were drunk. Maybe it was a little of both. An hour later we were all still in the game having traded money back and forth to a pretty even status. Then, the captain got a slight grin on his face and said "Hundred bucks" and threw the money in the pot.

I called the bet but the other 1LT raised 20 bucks. The chief warrant officer folded.

The captain then said, "I'll raise you 180 bucks to make it an even 300 dollars each in the pot!"

"Show us the money," said the 1LT.

The captain reached into his pocket for some script but apparently his pocket was empty.

"Look," he said, "I'm out of script and leaving tomorrow so I don't want to get more, I just want to cash yours in when I win this pot. I have this brand new FTQL 35mm Cannon camera with 12 rolls of unused film. I just paid 180 dollars for the camera out of the PACEX catalogue."

We all agreed to the bet. I used my last 200 dollars to match the pot and call. The 1LT had a pair of queens with an ace. The captain had three jacks and a pair of sixes. When I laid down my three kings and pair of 10s I thought that captain was going to cry.

Instead he laid out the biggest flurry of profanity I have ever heard. I picked up the pot of script and my new camera with 12 new rolls of film, walked back over to my gear and went to sleep.

Chapter Eighteen: The Air Cavalry

A Troop 7/17 Air Cavalry

From Saigon I caught a C130 plane to Phan Rang Air Base and flagged down an Army deuce and a half (military two and a half ton troop transport truck) that had 7/17 painted on the side and got a ride back to A Troop Headquarters.

The HQ was basically a non air-conditioned shack with a bunch of large tents and a few half assed wooden barracks surrounding it. Some of the shacks had air conditioners sticking out of the walls. As we drove up I noticed a line of soldiers giving what looked like urine samples.

"Aww crap," the driver yelled, "They're doing drug tests again!"

As we pulled up, all the troops in the back with me scattered every which way but toward the line of men. I picked up my duffle bag and reported to the HQ building for assignment. By now there was another WO1 from my training class with me, WO1 Ralph Graves. Ralph and I reported to Major Billy Miller.

Major Miller was suave and debonair. He wore a black cavalry hat slightly tilted.

"Damn," he said, "I told them NOT to send me over any new pilots right now. I've got all these damned ARVN pilots to train and you guys are going to get shit for flying time! They should have sent you up north. But since you're here, I will figure out what to do with you."

President Nixon and the ARVN Pilots

This was not good news for me and Ralph. We were both itching to get back behind the controls of a Huey. But this was a time of transition in Vietnam. President Nixon was determined to turn the war over to the South Vietnamese Army. And after the disaster of LAM SON 719 six months earlier he needed to get ARVN pilots some combat flight training. So Ralph and I would have to wait on our Huey flight time in Vietnam. We tried to settle in as best we could. I slept in a transient sleeping quarters with no air conditioning and a mosquito net over my bed. It was stiflingly hot 24 hours a day.

The makeshift Officers Club was attached to the same building as my sleeping room. It was made out of pieces of plywood and had an actual makeshift bar with four or five stools and a couple of tables. It looked hastily put together and in a condition that it could fall over any minute. It had no ice maker and no food. Just warm beer in steel cans (left over from the Korean War) and a few bottles of cheap scotch and vodka on the shelf. It was clearly a drinking only room.

But it was one of the rooms that had an air conditioner sticking out of the wall and was a respite from the unbearable heat and humidity. During the day it was empty. At evening time it would get very raucous as the air crews returned from their missions or from temporary overnight missions.

As the newest pilot and one that was not currently flying, I was the butt of jokes and harassment. Most of the "short timer" (pilots with fewer than three months left on their 12 month tour in Vietnam) pilots were the most seasoned and though they gave me some grief, the worst of it came from the boldest, bad ass, and ballsy pilots, the LOH drivers. These were the search and destroy (think go out and find the enemy and engage) pilots that flew low and slow in a Hughes OH-6 LOH (light observation helicopter). They saw the enemy "up close." You had to have balls to do that job and they let everyone know it. Especially the new guy... me. The LOH pilots made it their job to be obnoxious to all newbies and I was the current newest guy. I would not be for long.

About a week later I got my first unit introductory flight. Though I was not assigned to a flight platoon yet one of the ARVN pilots did not show up and the Aircraft Commander, a captain, needed a co-pilot.

He told me to just sit there and watch what he did. This mission was a standby for an ARVN unit and several American units that were withdrawing. We flew to a staging area which was a soccer field and shut the bird down.

The captain said, "Can't stand flying with those little ARVN dinks. They can't fly worth a shit."

It turned out that flight status, like many other positions in the ARVN Army, were political favors or family ties. A lot of men with little flying skills and abilities were sent to flight school and then expected to fly well in combat. That did not happen, as I would later find out in battle.

We didn't fly much that day and I was amazed at the Vietnamese children that would get close and encircle the helicopter. The rest of the crew didn't seem to mind but it made me nervous. How could you tell if they were VC?

The captain let me fly much of the rest of the mission, happy to have an American in the right seat. We only did one resupply to a small LZ (landing zone) that had an American team that needed C-rations (individual canned rations) and ammo.

The captain took the controls to show me how to get into that small landing zone. I was amazed at the twists and turns he put that helicopter through. This was not the type of approach that we were taught in flight school. Fast approach, very low level, and then pop up and flare hard and settle into the LZ. It was thrilling and it was also scary as hell. But the crew seemed to take it in their stride as if it was the only way they flew.

We were on the ground only a few seconds and the crew chief said, "Clear right, sir" then for the other side "Clear left," said the gunner. And up and away we went. It was my first real mission in Vietnam. I wondered how long it would take me to fly with the skill that the captain had demonstrated getting into that LZ.

Back at the dusty end of the Air Force base where the Cav was located I hit the bar that evening and had a warm beer.

The LOH pilots were in their usual condition and one looked at me and said, "Hey newbie, I hear you had your first mission and didn't kill anybody. Congratulations!" It was the kindest thing they had said in two weeks.

Chapter Nineteen:
Vietnam is a Crazy Place

O'Reilly and the Marijuana Deuce and a Half

One of the things that I quickly discovered at the Cav was that if you were not flying you were assigned an extra duty. This could be in the form of a new title like Tech Supply Officer or something more simple like "Mr. Crigler, we need an escort officer to accompany Sgt O'Reilly to Cam Ranh Bay for helicopter parts."

Now this would be pretty cool if I got my own Huey to fly O'Reilly to Cam Ranh Bay. But what Captain Whatshisname really meant was this: "O'Reilly is driving a deuce and a half. We will issue you both side arms. Oh, and Mr. Crigler, you better take along an M16 with some extra ammo. Oh, and don't be on that road after dark."

Now believe me, I'm thinking "Holy crap, I did not sign up for this, I'm a PILOT for Pete's sake!" But O'Reilly calms me down and tells me it's a routine run and that he's done this many times. He even requested the deuce and a half INSTEAD of a Huey. Reluctantly I checked out an M16 from the armory with a bandolier of ammo and hopped in the passenger seat.

Fortunately I remembered my 35mm camera. Out of the base we went, past the Air Force MP check station and onto the main road, Highway 1, and then north to Cam Ranh Bay. It was about an hour and a half ride according to O'Reilly.

The countryside was peaceful and serene. I took many pictures of the local Montagnard natives as we sped past. But I was certain that at any moment this crazy sergeant and out of place pilot would be attacked by the North Vietnamese. Thus my M16 was locked and loaded and my finger on the safety ready to go down fighting.

O'Reilly must have noticed my nervousness because after a few minutes he said, "Mr. Crigler. can I level with you?"

I said, "Sure O'Reilly, what's wrong?"

"Well, nothing really sir. I just want you to know that this is probably one of the safest roads around. It's guarded all the way to Cam Ranh Bay by the ARVN. And in my opinion sir, if the VC or NVA were anywhere around here those chicken shit ARVN would not be. So please don't point that M16 my way, sir."

I took my finger off the safety and relaxed a little.

Then he said, "Oh, one other thing sir. I have to make a stop at a little hooch up the way here. I need something to bargain with when we get to Cam Ranh Bay. The supply sergeant up there can't stand the Cav. We haven't been able to get decent parts for a while. One of our LOH pilots got drunk and pissed him off."

"That does not surprise me," I said.

"Anyway sir, we've been going through hell trying to get parts, especially tail rotors which the LOH pilots seem to like to destroy. But I know this guy and how he deals so I'm stopping at this hooch coming up, OK?"

Now this seemed a little odd to me but I went along with it anyway. I was certain that contraband must be involved somewhere in this story. After a mile or two we came to a small hut or hooch that appeared to NOT be surrounded by North Vietnamese. O'Reilly left the engine running and hopped out and disappeared into the hooch with hardly a knock. He had been there before. In a matter of two minutes out he comes with a plain paper bag, hops up in the driver's seat, puts the deuce and a half in gear and we are off to Cam Ranh Bay.

Not that I am without curiosity, and not to mention that I am a pilot without wings in the middle of Vietnam where there are NO FRONT LINES in a deuce and a half with a sergeant that is pulling a fast one.

"All right O'Reilly, what the fuck is going on? You didn't even hardly knock at that hooch and you were in and out in two minutes. What's in the bag, O'Reilly?"

"Sir, it's just a little negotiation equipment so that we can get a new LOH tail rotor that Mr. Bigly chewed up when he crashed his bird yesterday. He told me to do whatever was necessary to get some tail rotors," he said. "So I'm doing what I think is necessary, sir"

"What's in the bag O'Reilly?" I said.

"You're not going to quit asking me until you know for certain are you sir?" he said.

"No O'Reilly, I'm not."

"Well sir, you seemed pretty cool as a new WO1 to our unit. That is why I asked for you to be my escort officer. This is for the good of our unit sir so I'm just going to tell you… it's pot."

"What? You're shitting me right?" I said.

"No sir I'm not shitting you, it's POT sir. I know that the supply sergeant likes this stuff and I think I can get two tail rotor parts instead of one." he said.

Here I am, on my first escort mission as an officer and I have to get stuck in the middle of this. "This place is crazy," I thought.

"Let me think about this for a minute O'Reilly," I said.

"OK sir but please don't make me throw this stuff away as I don't think we can get the parts otherwise."

After a few minutes of bouncing down the road in that deuce and a half I looked over at O'Reilly and said, "OK sergeant, I haven't seen a thing. And you will tell that supply sergeant that I have not seen the contents of that paper bag. If this works we never talk about it again. If it doesn't, you are in some deep shit."

"Not a problem sir, it will work." he said.

Ten minutes later we pulled up to the guard gate at Cam Ranh Bay and then proceeded to the parts distribution area. I lit a cigarette or two while O'Reilly went in the back to work with the parts sergeant.

After about 10 minutes he came back with a big smile on his face.

"Sir, you won't believe this," he said, "We got 3 LOH tail rotor assemblies!"

We backed the deuce and a half around and they loaded the parts onto the back of the truck and off we went. For the entire trip back to Phan Rang O'Reilly had a shit eating grin on his face. We got back about an hour before dusk and pulled over to the technical supply shack for A Troop.

I looked over at O'Reilly and said, "Good job sergeant," and proceeded to the makeshift Officers Club to get a warm beer and my nightly ration of new guy harassment.

The next day as I was walking past the HQ shack Major Miller saw me and hollered, "Mr. Crigler, come over here."

I walked over to Maj Miller and he said, "Mr. Crigler we've been trying to get extra parts from Cam Ranh Bay for weeks. And in one parts run you get three very difficult to get rotor assemblies. How did you do it mister?"

"Sir, I just let my NCO do all the talking, sir. Sergeant O'Reilly did a good job," I said.

"Well, O'Reilly is telling everyone that you are the reason we got so many parts. It doesn't matter though, good job Mr. Crigler. We'll see if we can get you flying soon."

Drug Tests

As I walked away from Maj Miller I saw another line of soldiers waiting to give urine samples. In 1972 there were no drug tests available for marijuana but they did have tests for opium and heroin which were both readily available in Vietnam. And our unit, like most in Vietnam, had men that turned to harder drugs to escape, at least mentally, the war.

I knew of no pilots that used drugs, other than alcohol. But I had no idea about the gunners, crew chiefs, and ground personnel. It was my first view of the morale problems that the war and loss of civilian support back home was causing. It would not be the last.

Tech Supply

A couple days later Maj Miller gave me a reward of sorts. Since I had done such a good job getting the parts in Cam Ranh Bay, Maj Miller decided that I should have the dubious distinction of being the unit tech supply officer as an extra duty. I was not happy as this job was one that NO other pilot wanted because it could reduce flight time. But I had no choice.

Besides, most of us new pilots were getting bumped from flight time anyway due to the big push to train the ARVN pilots.

It also turned out that most of the tech supply duty was handled by a sergeant. His name was Lawrence L. Lawrence and his middle initial stood for Lawrence. Sergeant Lawrence Lawrence Lawrence was a strange bird. He was a Canadian citizen that lived just across the river from Detroit, Michigan in Windsor, Canada. But he worked in the U.S. and apparently that made him eligible for the U.S. Draft. When his draft notice arrived he accepted his fate and entered the Army.

Most of my civilian friends would have told him to just stay in Canada. But Lawrence loved the U.S. And as he had an excellent memory he was perfect for managing the organization of aircraft parts. He knew where to find every part. Lawrence would demonstrate his memory abilities by reciting all the U.S. states in alphabetical order and name the capitals both forward and in reverse order. He amazed me. And he managed everything. He had little need for me other than the occasional requisition that needed an officer's signature.

Chapter Twenty: Conscientious Objector

Brother Mike

I had now been at A Troop for about three or four weeks. The heat was miserable at night and without a fan or air conditioning it was difficult to sleep. So I decided to take a trip to the Air Force side of the base and see if I could procure a small fan to put at the base of my bed inside the mosquito netting to give me some air movement.

It turned out that the Air Force actually had a Post Exchange or PX on the base and rumor had it that they sold small fans. I also wanted to see my brother Mike who I had not seen for over a year. So I hitched a ride on a Jeep heading towards the PX. I was amazed at how good the Air Force had it in Vietnam versus the Army Cavalry. We lived in dust and heat. The Air Force had air-conditioned barracks, great chow halls, well-built officers and NCO clubs and all of it looked as if it was back in the States.

The jeep dropped me off at the PX and I quickly purchased a small fan and some 35mm film for my camera. Then I walked about two blocks over to a large concrete block barrack that had a sign that said MP unit on it.

I walked in the front door, strolled up to the guard desk and said, "I'm looking for Mike Crigler, I think he's an MP in this unit. Can you help me?"

"Sure," do you have a delivery for him?" he said, looking at my fan and bag of film.

"No, he's my brother and I'm stationed at A Troop on the edge of your base and wanted to say hello to him," I said.

"You're Crigler's brother? An officer? A pilot?" he said, looking at my wings and Warrant Officer bars.

"Yes I am."

"Well things never cease to amaze me," he said. "Your brother is confined to his quarters except for chow. He's advised our commanding officer that he is a 'conscientious objector' to the war and refuses to carry a weapon."

"No fucking way," I said.

"No sir, true as can be. We are going to ship him out in a week or two," he said.

"Well, is he allowed visitors?"

"Sure sir, let me go get him and you two can spend some time in his confined quarters."

Mike was so happy to see me he cried. For me, I was absolutely astounded at his room. He had his own private room and it was better than Maj Miller's quarters. Air-conditioned, a thick mattress with clean linen sheets, a desk, and posters of Jimmy Hendrix and John Lennon everywhere.

"Jim," he said, "this war sucks and we are in it for all the wrong reasons. That's why I've declared myself as a conscientious objector. The Air Force will have to send me back to the States and give me a general discharge. But I don't care. I'm not fighting in this war."

I was saddened by this news but respected Mike's opinion on the war. We talked for about 20 minutes and then I ran out of cigarettes.

"Mike you got a smoke?" I said.

"Sure Jim, take one of these," and he tossed me a pack of Kool cigarettes.

I pulled one out of the pack and lit it. I wasn't a menthol cigarette smoker but I was out cigarettes so this would have to do. We continued to talk and suddenly I noticed that I was getting high.

"Mike, what's in this cigarette?" I said.

"Holy fuck, sorry Jim I gave you the wrong pack! "Stuck in this room all day I occasionally get high, and that ain't pot."

"Damn it Mike," I said as the room started to spin. "I could lose my wings over this shit! How could you do this?"

It was getting late and I needed to get back to my unit but when I stood up I could hardly walk. "I don't even want to know what was in that smoke but you have to help me get back to my unit," I said.

"Wait a minute Jim, take a swig of this," and he handed me a bottle of Southern Comfort.

"What are you talking about, I can't walk as it is," I said.

"Look Jim, you just need to 'smell' like alcohol. I'll tell them I got you drunk."

So I took a swig of whiskey, swished it around my mouth and spit it in his trash can. Mike then helped me up, grabbed my fan and film and walked me out stumbling past the guard.

"What the fuck is up with him? He can't even walk and he's only been in your room about 30 minutes!" the guard said to Mike.

"He's upset that I'm a conscientious objector and he drank my Southern Comfort," Mike said.

The guard walked over to me, got close to my face, and sniffed.

"Holy crap, did he drink the whole bottle?"

"Almost," Mike said.

"Damn, I heard those Cav warrant officers like to drink a lot. Better get him out by the road so he can catch a ride back to his unit," the guard said.

And with that Mike helped me out to the road. About two minutes later he flagged a deuce and a half with 7/17 markings on the door. There was a group of soldiers in the back coming from the NCO club.

Mike said, "Hey this warrant officer is with your unit, can you help me get him up in the truck and give him a lift? He's a little drunk."

Several of the troops got out and threw me up into the deuce and a half. I landed in a heap in the back of the truck bed. But in my condition I felt no pain. Mike waved farewell and I gave him a wave back. It would be the last time I saw my brother until I returned from Vietnam. But in the back of the deuce and a half all of the privates and sergeants were eyeing me up.

I just looked at them and said, "Southern Comfort! Stay away from that shit, that's an order!"

They all laughed and didn't say another word. I must have been their first inebriated officer.

Air Conditioning at Last

I was lucky as Army officers were NOT typically required to take urine drug tests. I did not drink alcohol for two weeks after that incident. And I never bummed another cigarette from ANYONE ever again.

In the mean time I settled into my extra duty as a tech supply officer. After about a week I was invited to join two other warrant officers that worked in maintenance to share their hooch. It was air conditioned and it even had a makeshift shower. Holy cow this was heaven.

Slow Flying

But even though I had an air-conditioned place to sleep, I was still miserable! I was a pilot and I wanted to fly. Instead of getting 100 or more hours per month we were lucky to get 20. So I would volunteer for ANY flight. If I could not get flight time in a Huey then I would volunteer as an observer in a LOH (Observers Sit in the co-pilot seat of an OH-6 with an M16 and help spot enemy positions and return fire).

I could not fly on station because I was not transitioned to an OH-6 but the pilots would let me fly to and from the staging areas. At least I was flying.

I would also volunteer for any test flights or relocation flights. I actually got 20 hours in the front seat of a Cobra Gunship. But the flying, due to the ARVN training orders, would be slow for the first three months.

Chapter Twenty One:

The Great 129th Heist

129th Typhoon

One day we had several assault helicopter units fly into Phan Rang Air Base from further north up the Vietnam coast due to a typhoon forecasted to hit their area. These guys were bringing their Hueys down to keep them protected from the winds. And all of the pilots that I met seemed pretty happy due to no combat flying for a couple days. And to top it off the Air Force put them up in their transient officers' quarters which were POSH compared to normal Army units.

The typhoon came and went and so did the units that flew in. But for me it was the same. Showing up at the tech supply shack, talking to Lawrence Lawrence Lawrence. Signing a few requisitions. Then Lawrence Lawrence Lawrence would quiz me on the states and their respective capitals. Then I would go hang out at the flight line and beg for flight time.

Finally, after a few near misses with ARVN pilots, some of the aircraft commanders started looking for excuses to fly with the new warrants like me. I started getting tagged as a co-pilot more than before. I also was getting to know some of the pilots better. One day, after a total of eight hours flying time on some particularly long missions, the warrant officer aircraft commander that I flew with invited me to the Air Force Officers Club for a couple drinks and a burger. We grabbed a Jeep and drove the mile and a half to the O Club.

I was still amazed at how good the Air Force had it in Vietnam. This O Club was as good as any I had seen back in the States! But as we walked in some of the Air Force brass at the bar gave us the stink eye.

"Army pilots are not welcome in here," said one of the Lieutenants at the bar.

"What gives?" said the A/C that I was with. "We come here pretty regularly. Oh, and you guys are ALWAYS welcome at our club!" he said.

"Well, the base commander is considering making our club facilities off limits to Army personnel."

Then a captain that was with him looked at us and said, " You guys have no idea what happened last week do you?"

"Not a clue," said the A/C.

"Well, it seems that a bunch of your guys from the 129th Assault Helicopter Company were put up in our transient officers and enlisted barracks until the typhoon blew past their base in An Son. First of all, what a bunch of barbarous sons of bitches. We never saw so many fights in our NCO Lounge (Non-commissioned officer or enlisted soldiers' lounge). And several of your drunken warrant officers tried to pick a fight with one of our colonels and several majors. Called them a bunch of REMFs (Rear Echelon Mother Fuckers)," he said. "But the worst of it is when the club closed, they broke back in and stole some booze and about half of our bar stools."

Sure as hell, as we looked on about half the stools were missing.

The captain continued, "But the absolute most hellacious part, and the part that put the commander over the top was that they stole EVERYTHING from the officers transient quarters. Beds, linens, air conditioners, lighting. They even took a sink off the wall!"

"Holy Crap," the A/C chimed in. "Since we live on this base and 'theoretically' are on your side, can we order a beer while we listen to this?"

"Sure, barkeep get two beers for these crazy helicopter pilots. They live here," he said. "But there's more," he said.

The aircraft commander and I sipped an ice cold beer. I had not had anything but warm beer in a long time and the Army beer was left over beer in pallets from the Korean War. It was in rusty steel cans. This beer was in bottles and fairly fresh. Damn, did it taste good.

"They put everything in their helicopters and covered the windows with white stuff (we used a white paste to clean the Plexiglas window and if you wiped it on and did not wipe it off, it would leave a white haze on the window). Then they took off in three groups. We didn't find out about the thefts until they'd been gone for about 30 minutes. The commanding officer was going to scramble the jets and shoot 'em down but the executive officer convinced him to instead call up the food chain to the Army brass," he said. "Then all hell broke loose with verbal accusations going back and forth. The Army general said he'd look into it. So I'm just saying to you two Army warrant officers, if the commander walks in this place I would advise you to lay low."

My A/C looked at him and said, "Well damn, thanks for the heads up!"

Then he ordered us two more cold beers and a burger.

I found out later the Army general tracked down just one of the formation flights going up the coast. They were ordered to immediately land at a close-by Army base for inspection. However, as the flight was on long final approach for landing over the South China sea someone said they thought they saw bedding being thrown into the sea as those choppers came in mighty low and slow.

The inspection took place without incident and the general was notified that no contraband was found on the helicopters. Thus began a rather strained relationship with the Air Force at Phan Rang.

Chapter Twenty Two: If You Ain't CAV, You Ain't Shit!

Cavalry Hat and Initiation into the Air Cavalry

As the weeks rolled by I was tapped more and more for co-pilot duty. My two maintenance officer roommates thought I was nuts.

"The unit is tagged to stand down soon Crigler, why expose yourself?" they would say. "Rumor has it that the war is going to be over soon. There's not been a lot of action for the last four or five months and some of the brass up the chain of command think the Paris Peace talks are having an effect."

"Look you guys," I said, "I came over here to fly, NOT sit behind a desk! I want to fly like the best aircraft commanders we have."

But they were right, there was a lull in the war in late 1971. Oh we had rocket attacks and we took plenty of hits in our aircraft. But we did not see the major battles like were shown on TV back in the States.

I speculated that the North Vietnamese were just letting President Nixon pull out all the troops before they made another big assault. Months later I would find out how right I was. But now, and in spite of their persistence, I continued to volunteer for any flight.

Many pilots in the Air Cavalry wore black Stetson Cavalry hats, many decorated with their rank and insignia, just like Major Miller. It was a status symbol of sorts that had to be earned. One of the new guys told me that you had to be in the unit for four months OR get your cherry busted (take enemy fire at your helicopter). Although being forced in to the tech supply business as an extra duty did not enamor me to like the Cavalry, I was interested in earning one of those Cavalry hats.

As the weeks went by and my flying skills improved I flew on more missions. Typically it was the same thing each time. We would fly the Huey to a staging area, usually a secure field or soccer field. Shut the bird down and wait orders. Many of the missions were in support of the LOH and Cobra teams in case of enemy contact of LOH problems (think tail rotor in the trees).

We also flew a lot of insertions of ARVN Troopers. The crew took the attitude that if the ARVNs wanted us to insert them into an area the VC or North Vietnamese surely were NOT there. I did not care what their cavalier attitude was; I hid as far below my chicken plate small arms seat armor as I could on each insertion. I got pretty good at scrunching behind those armor plates and still able to fly well.

As time went on though, I concentrated more on flying than hiding behind that chicken plate.

During one of those insertions we were allowing the ARVN to repel into the tree canopy.

"Sir, I think we're taking fire to our 3 o'clock. I don't see rounds but I can hear an AK47."

The A/C had me at the controls doing a high hover trying to be stationary until the troops were down.

"Just hold it steady Crigler and keep this altitude. Just a couple more left to repel," he said.

"Roger, will do," I said.

"Last two ARVN ready to repel sir," said the gunner.

Just then, "BANG." A round hit my door just above my head just as the troopers exited the bird to repel down.

The A/C said, "Take 'er down a couple feet and hold the hover Jim."

"Roger," I said.

"They're both down, sir," said the crew chief.

"Right, now get those ropes in quick. All right Crigler, I have the aircraft."

"Roger, you have the aircraft," I said.

With that, the captain pulled pitch and we got the hell out of there. I was soaked in sweat. It was bad enough trying to stationary high hover without much horizon reference, but with bullets flying you had a tendency to tighten up. This is not good as flying a helicopter is much like playing a fine instrument. The touch is light and you are one with the bird. I did not think that I did a good job.

The A/C didn't say much on the way back. This was our last mission of the day and we were on our way back to Phan Rang.

When we arrived the captain said, "I need to be at the operations shack right away. Crigler, shut this bird down and I'll meet you at the bar to debrief."

"Roger that captain," I said.

I went through the shutdown procedures of the Huey one by one until finally the blades stopped and the crew chief tied the blades off to the tail. As I was getting out of the bird the gunner and crew chief came over to the front of the bird.

The chief said, "Nice job today Mr. Crigler."

Then the gunner said, "Sir, congratulations on getting your cherry busted. It's time to order that Cav hat!"

"Thanks," I said. I hadn't even thought of that until just then. "I will definitely order my Cav hat as soon as possible!" I said.

I stowed my flight helmet in the maintenance officers room and turned my pistol into the armory and walked over to the makeshift Cavalry bar. There were already pilots at the bar and as I walked in a hush came over the room.

The captain that was my A/C that day stepped out from behind the bar and said, "A toast! To our newest newbie cherry buster!"

And with that they all raised a glass. Then one of the LOH pilots walked over and dumped a glass of beer on my head.

"Congratulations newbie!" he said. "Bartender, all his drinks are on me tonight."

And the alcohol flowed. The captain told the story about five times of how I hovered so cool and calm in the face of enemy fire. I'm glad he left the part about my soaking wet from sweat flight suit out of the story. The pilots never harassed me again.

That night the captain gave me a paper order form from the Stetson Hat Company which I then filled out in military script and attached 20 dollars to. He had one of the HQ enlisted men make the order for me the next day. Three weeks later I got my brand new black Cavalry Stetson hat. But wearing this hat would be another issue.

Drink the GMF

Back at my hooch I took the hat out of the box and put it on. It looked pretty good in the mirror. But one of my roommates, Warrant Officer Paul Duryea said, "You know that you can't wear that fucker until you get initiated don't you?"

"What are you talking about Paul? I got my cherry busted for God's sake!"

"Look Jim, rules are rules. You can't wear that hat until you drink the GMF."

"What's a GMF?" I said.

"Well, look, the Cav has formal initiations at the Air Force Officers Club during the intermissions of the USO shows. Well, they call them USO shows but they're really just Vietnamese bands with some Vietnamese strippers. At their half time break we have our initiation and then you get to find out what the GMF is. In the meantime put that hat back in the box. There is a USO show in a couple days. I'm sure you'll be fine," he said.

Now Duryea was known to be a prankster. He was always doing things like making "potato guns" out of Pepsi cans and using zippo lighter fluid as propellant. He would lob potatoes with his potato gun over to the Air Force guard shack 50 or so yards from our perimeter, trying to scare the guards and keep them on their toes. Or so he said.

But this time he was not joking with me. The captain looked me up later that day and told me NOT to wear the hat until after initiation which would be in a couple of days. I was one of three new warrants getting initiated and he was sure the Air Force O Club would be the place.

He said, "Major Miller just has to have a conversation with the commander over there after those fucking 129th guys pissed him off so bad."

"Ok captain, no sweat. Say captain, what is a GMF?"

"A GMF?" he said. "Oh, you mean for the initiation. That's short for Green Mother Fucker. You'll like it Crigs. The barkeeper gets a one pound coffee can and puts a shot of everything on the bar in it until it's about a half inch from the top. Then they fill it the rest of the way with green crème de menthe. Thusly becoming that famous Cavalry initiation drink known as the Green Mother Fucker!"

And so, there it was... the GMF. I would think about it for days. I wish I hadn't asked.

Fortunately I was flying for the next couple of days so I didn't have to sit in the tech supply office and think about it. But finally the big night came. In spite of the fact that the Air Force officers did not like the Army pilots, we would invade their USO show anyway. It was actually kind of cool to walk in to the Air Force O Club with a bunch of Army pilots wearing Cavalry hats and take over the club.

And take over we did. We were rowdy and obnoxious at the band and especially the cheap strippers. At half time, myself and two other wobbly ones were called to the stage. One of the captains read off a proclamation of Cavalry initiation and read each of our names while three other officers delivered the official GMFs to each of us.

Then, Cavalry hat in our left hand and Green Mother Fuckers in our right hand, we all lifted the coffee can up high in air and toasted in unison, "IF YOU AIN'T CAV, YOU AIN'T SHIT!"

And then each of us put our lips to that coffee can and started gulping. You couldn't just drink it or you would start to gag. If that happened it was all over and you were puking in your hat. But I just gulped away until I finally reached the end. In fact, we all ended at about the same time. We lifted those cans up in the air and tipped them over so that the crowd of cheering pilots could see that we had indeed drunk it to the bottom. Then, all three of us put our Cavalry hats on and walked off that stage.

Flying close formation 7/17 Air Cavalry

Now the O Club band area was outside in the open air and had a railing all around two sides. Rows of chairs were set up with an aisle down the middle leading to the back railing. This railing overlooked the Air Force officers' quarters. And that is precisely where the three of us headed. You see, one could not possibly drink that much alcohol and survive, or keep it down for that matter.

When we reached the railing all you could see was three warrant officer pilots projectile vomiting towards the Air Force officers' quarters. A few swishes of water in the mouth and we put our Stetsons back on our heads and promptly rejoined our group of pilots and finished the striptease show. Even though we vomited up all that booze, some of the alcohol still got in our systems. I had no idea how I got back to my room that night.

Chapter Twenty Three: Ready to Stand Down

Sporadic Flying

Duryea woke me up early the next morning. My head was pounding.

"Crigler, get up! You need to fly with Mr. Olson. He's tapped you as his co-pilot."

Of all the days I would want to fly, this was not one of them. But fly we did. CW2 Olson was at the initiation last night too. So I got up, threw some water on my face, lit a smoke and went to meet Olson in the operations shack.

"Easy stuff Crigs," he said. "We have a mission over by Buon Ma Thuot to fly some ARVN brass and a U.S. advisor around. Grab your weapons out of the armory and help PFC Norman, the gunner, carry those extra C-rations. We may need them."

I grabbed an M16 with a bandolier of ammo and my 38 pistol. Then I walked over to Norman and grabbed a case of C-rations and we headed to the ship. While Olson was getting briefed with call signs and radio frequencies, I grabbed a can of "eggs and cheese" out of one of the C-ration cases. I needed some food in me to get rid of this hangover. It would not be the last time I flew in this condition.

Olson let me start the Huey up to operational RPM and then he said, "OK you guys, we have some good missions. Probably flyovers so some ARVN brass and a U.S. advisor can see some area they want to evaluate. Mr. Crigler, back us out of this revetment and take us over to the runway for takeoff."

I always liked flying with the warrant officers vs the RLOs (real live officers... think captain, lieutenant, major) because they wanted us to learn by doing to get the confidence of flying. I slowly backed us out and hovered over to the runway.

"Alright Crigs, take off and head towards this heading and wake me up in 20 minutes," he said pointing his hand in a westward direction. And with that he lit a cigarette, took a couple of puffs and promptly napped at 3000 feet for about 45 minutes. I flew us all the way to Buon Ma Thuot.

Olson woke up, lit a cigarette and said, "Alright Crigs, I have the aircraft, nice job. Damn I needed that nap!"

I was thinking the same thing. I lit a smoke and relaxed while Olson took us on final approach to the compound at Buon Ma Thuot.

We shut the bird down and Olson and I were escorted to a briefing area. The U.S. advisor was a major and he gave us a brief synopsis of our day ahead.

"Okay guys, we think the NVA are building up forces in this area," he said pointing to coordinates on a map. "We have ARVN rangers in this area and they are seeing lots of buildup activity. We think something's up in the next month or two."

It was late December 1971, just prior to Christmas. Throughout the day we landed at several ARVN outposts. They were very similar to our U.S. outposts as they were surrounded by barbed wire and had Claymore mines facing outward in case of attack. At one of these outposts I saw a pile of bodies. Many were mangled pretty badly, missing arms and legs. One had his face blown entirely off. These men were Viet Cong that had attempted to infiltrate the base and attack the ammo dump the night before. This was my first gruesome view of war dead. It would not be my last.

Christmas in Vietnam

A few days after my missions with Olson I woke up to Duryea humming several Christmas songs.

"Wake up Crigler, it's Christmas," he said, Tossing me a rusty steel can of Budweiser he said, "Here, I got you a present. What did you get for me?"

I looked at the Budweiser and tossed it back to him.

"I'm re-gifting this Bud back to you. I know how much you like Budweiser."

I was not in a Christmas mood. And I was terribly lonely and missed my family. I hadn't received a letter from my family or friends for three or four weeks. It was getting to the point that I was the first one at mail call and the last one to leave. 99% of the time I got no letter.

I never experienced a Christmas as lonely as that one. I wrote several letters home then went to our makeshift Cav bar and drank a few scotches and water. It tasted much better than the beer in steel cans. At the bar some of the pilots were talking about all the rumors flying around about 7/17 Cav standing down. It was looking more and more like I would be going home from Vietnam early.

Believe me; I was ready to go home.

Chapter Twenty Four:
1LT Tom Shaw

A Protestant Mass with a Catholic Rosary

The Army would occasionally send a chaplain to the unit to talk with the troops and hold a service. You never knew what denomination the chaplain was until he showed up. Around the second week of January 1972 we had one such chaplain show up. He was a Lutheran minister and planned a service for 9am on Sunday.

The war was still in a sort of lull regarding any major battles. Just the occasional harassment of 120mm rockets or mortars at night and the ever present AK47 fire we occasionally took with missions to support the ARVN. But I wasn't taking any chances as none of us knew if a bullet with our name on it was the next to hit us.

I decided to go to the Lutheran service and ask the Lord for a little protection. It was the first service that I had attended in Vietnam. While I was praying with the rest of the troops and listening to the Lutheran minister, I pulled my Grandma's rosary out of my right calf pocket on my flight suit and started to pray the beads. It was towards the end of the service and I had not said a rosary in many years. But I thought, "What the hell, it can't hurt."

1LT Tom Shaw

As the service ended I still had a few "Hail Mary"s and "Our Father"s to pray on the rosary so I sat in one of the folding chairs and took about five minutes to finish.

When I stood up to leave a voice behind said, "Hey Catholic!"

I turned to see a 1LT who must have been watching me walk over with his hand extended.

"Tom Shaw from Fond du Lac, Wisconsin," he said as he shook my hand. "Only a Catholic would pray the rosary at a Lutheran service."

I laughed, "Yeah, well I was very Catholic when I was younger, now any church will do. My Grandma gave me this rosary for good luck so I thought it couldn't hurt to at least pray the beads for some safe luck."

Tom advised me that he had just gotten to the unit the previous day. He had gotten a Cobra transition right out of flight school but when he got to 7/17 Cav they had assigned him to be a maintenance officer. They told him to look for Warrant Officer Crigler or Duryea. He had come up to the service to pray and it was just happenstance that I was the first person that he would meet.

About two weeks prior, the CW2 that shared our room had completed his one year tour and returned to the States. Tom was looking for a place to sleep and call home.

"Sure, we have a spare bed," I said. "The other maintenance officer just finished his tour. Follow me and I will introduce you to WO1 Duryea. But I must warn you, he does not think highly of RLOs."

"What's an RLO?" Tom Said.

"It's warrant officer slang for real live officer. Most of us warrants think you guys had it pretty easy going through flight school and not getting the shit harassed out of you by a TAC officer trying to get you to break," I said.

"Thanks for the warning," Tom said.

I walked Tom down to the maintenance hooch where we bedded down. As we walked up to the door Tom noticed a stenciled message painted on the door: "If you are a captain, don't bother to knock, we don't want to talk to you anyway."

"You weren't kidding about the RLO thing were you?" Tom said.

"Nope. But don't worry, Duryea is harmless," I said.

I introduced Tom to WO1 Paul Duryea and Paul was quite cordial. I guess if you're going to room with someone you don't want to start the relationship off with a negative note. And Duryea, being a native from Louisiana, could be very cordial. We all laughed off the stenciled note on the door.

Tom said, "I like that stencil. I've known some captains that are wound way too tight. Happy to have that note on the door."

Tom and I, being from large Catholic families, had many things in common. Since there wasn't a lot of flying going on we had plenty of time to talk. Tom was the oldest of five and was married to his wife Ann and had a young son, Tom Jr. We talked about our lives back home and got to know each other pretty well. We were instant friends. But I kept my moral dilemma to myself. Still after all this time I did not know what direction to take with that part of my life.

But where Tom and I differed greatly was in our stability of life. I had never gone to the same school more than two years in my entire life and moved to a new home nine times before I graduated high school. Tom lived in the same house growing up and went through the same schooling system. He had a stable set of parents and spoke highly of his father. He seemed to have a different "life compass" than I did. I would later call it his "moral compass."

Chapter Twenty Five:

129th Assault Helicopter Company – Bulldogs

The 7/17th Cav was doing very little flying in January 1972. It seemed like they were just packing up. And that's exactly what they were doing. The official word came down and Major Miller announced that the unit was standing down from combat and returning to Ft Hood, Texas.

There was a lot of excitement during this announcement, until he said, "For those of you wondering if you are joining us on the trip back to Texas, here is the cut off. If you have more than 180 days in combat zone, you're going home. The rest of you will be assigned to other units in Vietnam that are short on pilots and crew."

I had a little more than four months in country. Duryea would be going home. Tom and I would be reassigned. Five days later Tom and I received our transfer orders. We were assigned to the 129th Assault Helicopter Company based in An Son. This was about 100 miles north along the coast and very near a coastal city called Qui Nhon.

Also assigned to the 129th were WO1 Ralph Graves and PFC Ferrell Norman. I had flown with Norman as my gunner many times in the Cav. That night at the bar one of the warrant officers that was going home got into a discussion with me on the Air Cavalry vs other units. He had been with a different unit that stood down several months ago and was transferred to the 7/17th but was now going home. Because of this he had not qualified for a Cavalry hat.

Being a little indifferent to the Cav and not very happy with being set aside in tech supply while the ARVN pilots got all the flight time, I was not attached to my Cavalry hat or the Air Cavalry. I offered him my hat for the same price I had paid for it, about 25 dollars. He gladly accepted it as a trophy since he did not qualify for the initiation. Years later I would regret selling that hat.

The next day we processed out of the unit and caught a C-130 transport to Qui Nhon air strip. From there a 129th Huey picked us up and we flew to Lane Army Heliport in An Son about a 10 minute flight away. From the air this was much different than Phan Rang as this was strictly an Army helicopter base with no long runway for large fixed wing aircraft to land.

I didn't count the helicopters on the ground but there must have been over 100. It was also different in that it was pure Army. We were not a dusty bump on the side of an Air Force compound. The pilot landed us near an operations shack. We unloaded our gear and headed to the 129th Headquarters. There we met Major Alan Jones.

Major Jones was not as suave and cocky as Major Miller with his cavalry hat. But Major Jones was welcoming and got right down to business.

"Gentlemen, we are happy to have you! We've got some seasoned pilots heading back to the States and we need some replacement co-pilots," he said. "I see you two spent some time in maintenance. Crigler you were actually a tech supply officer."

My heart sank as I waited for him discuss the dreaded maintenance officer role. I'm sure Tom was thinking the same thing.

"Well, those roles are currently filled in our unit so right now there are no extra duties to assign to either of you. Lieutenant Shaw, I see you have a Cobra transition. We have no open Cobra slots as we currently have more Cobra pilots that we can use. That may change later," he said. "In the mean time you guys will be flying. Crigler, I'm assigning you to the 1st Flight Platoon. Shaw you will co-pilot for 2nd Flight Platoon."

You could see the relief on both of our faces. I was ecstatic. I would now be doing what I was trained to do. FLY!

The Major dismissed us and an orderly took us to the temporary officers' quarters so we could have a bed for the night. It was non air-conditioned and hot. At least I had my fan to move the air around.

I didn't care though. I had landed in a real flying unit.

Buy a Room from WO1 No-name

The next morning after chow I met my new platoon leader, Captain John Goodnight. He was cordial enough and happy to have me in his flight platoon.

"You will probably know some of the guys in our platoon as you graduated in the same flight class," he said. "WO1 Faucher and WO1 Bramel I believe were in your same class."

"Yes sir, I know them both," I said.

"Good, those guys are both good pilots; let's see if you can keep your flight class standing. Be ready to fly with me in an hour. I will take you out for a unit check ride. We've got some resupply to do in the area and it's a good time for you to fly with me," he said.

"Roger that, sir," I said.

An hour later I was in the right seat of Huey 593. Sp4 Gary Woodward was the crew chief on this bird. Captain Goodnight let me start up the ship and back it out of the revetment. Then I hovered over for takeoff and called the tower.

"Roger, cleared for takeoff 593," came the reply.

Goodnight pointed in a westward direction and said, "Take her up to 1500 feet, we are flying over the Tiger compound to pick up some troops and supplies for the Korean outposts."

He took over the aircraft on final approach to show me where we would be landing. Then we loaded up with K-rations (Korean C-rations with Korean type food), ammo, and lots of plastic jerry can water jugs.

We also picked up a Korean interpreter that the captain called an RTO (Radio Translation Operator). From there we would do two or three re-supplies of Korean outposts per pick up. Some outposts were large with a company of men, others were on mountaintops with just a small contingent of troops. The 129th was their lifeline for supplies.

As I flew the captain would point out landmarks and tell me to make a mental note.

"When the weather gets bad you will be glad you remembered those markers," he said.

■ *First Flight Platoon 129th AHC. WO1 Crigler in cargo bay (center)*

We flew the rest of the day resupplying outposts. Each time we would complete a drop off the captain would make another hash mark on the windshield with his grease pencil. Most of the resupply missions were pretty easy. But some were downright scary as you might have to land on a mountain peak with barely enough room for the skids of the helicopter to fit on the landing site. Plus, the winds could be very treacherous and swirl from all directions. The captain pointed out that we always burn off some fuel weight before attempting these landings.

"It gives us a little more margin for error," he said.

That afternoon when we got back to Lane Heliport Captain Goodnight checked me off to fly co-pilot.

He counted up the grease pencil hash marks on the window and said, "22 missions today. About average." Then he looked at me and said, "Starting tomorrow you will rotate as co-pilot between aircraft commanders in my platoon. You get to learn something from everybody. You will be getting a lot more flight time here than you did with the 7/17th."

I felt good being in this platoon. And Captain Goodnight was as good a pilot as I had seen in Vietnam.

Back at the room I discovered that Tom had gone through a similar day with his platoon leader. Except that he admitted that he was pretty rusty having not flown a Huey in several months. I forgot, he was a real "newbie". We decided to head over to the O Club to check it out.

The Officers Club at Lane was nowhere near as nice as the Air Force club. But it was a thousand times better than the Cavalry plywood shack. It had a long bar with some very familiar Air Force bar stools. Also a crap table, a ping pong table, and lots of tables for playing cards. There seemed to be a lot of guys playing bridge. It also had Vietnamese bar maids. Though this was surprising to me it was also a pleasant surprise to see pretty women in a war zone.

Tom and I had talked previously about sharing a room together. So we started talking to the pilots that we met and asking if any of them were about to end their tour in Vietnam to see if their room was available.

Pretty soon a WO1 who will go un-named walked up to us and said, "If you guys are looking for a room I have the best one in the unit. And I'm leaving in two days. You want to see it?"

"Absolutely," we said.

As we walked out of the club we faced a walkway with small buildings (hooches) on each side of the walkway, maybe five buildings on each side. The third building on the left was his. On the outside it looked like all the rest, with sandbags on the roof and 55 gallon drums filled with sand surrounding the building in case of mortar or rocket attack. On the inside as we entered there was a hallway with a sink at the end. Just to the right as you entered was a shower stall with a 55 gallon drum filled with water above the shower.

"Just turn the spigot sticking out of the bottom of the barrel and you can get enough water to shower. As long as the generator is working we can get water pumped in. If you are lucky it's warm from the sun, otherwise it's cold showers. But you won't mind," he said.

There were two small rooms on the right side next to the shower and a door on the left side of the hall. At the end of the hall there was a sink that looked like it had been ripped out of a wall and just stuck there. The WO1 opened the door on the left and we walked into his room.

It took up half the building. It had a refrigerator and a full bar. Above that was a loft bed. There was another bed below the loft on the floor. And it was air-conditioned. As I looked around I noticed USAF stenciled on the lighting and air conditioning. The room also had nice thick mattresses like the one my brother had in his Air Force room.

"Where did you get all this stuff?" I asked.

"Well, let's just say that our friends in the Air Force donated it to us. That's all that needs to be said, OK?" he said.

Then the WO1 walked over behind the bar and said, "One other thing. There are some special features to this room. I have a date here tonight and she's in this wall."

"What?!" Tom said.

"Yeah, I only have two nights left and I have a date tonight," he said.

With that he slid a piece of paneling up to reveal a small hiding room behind the bar. It even had lighting. Out came a little Vietnamese prostitute with a big smile on her face.

"It's alright Kim, I'm just showing these guys the room, go back and I will get you out shortly," he said to the girl. And back into the false wall she went.

"I see nothing," I said.

"Can't you get in trouble for that?" Tom said.

"Not as long as you guys don't say anything I can't. Now, are you interested in buying the room or not?" he said.

"Buying?" Tom said.

"Yeah buying. This room is 300 bucks. That's how much I have in it. Not to mention the sweat equity and the hidden room. By the way, the girl does not come with it. But I will leave the two bottles of scotch in the bar. They were given to my ex-roommate Festus and he doesn't drink scotch."

Tom Shaw looked at me. I looked around the room and looked back at Tom.

"I've got 150 bucks if you do", I said.

Tom looked at the WO1 and said, "Done deal, mister. We'll move in day after tomorrow."

And with that we each pulled out 150 dollars in military script and bought our room.

■ *WO1 Crigler in his and Tom Shaw's $300 hooch*

Tom is my Roommate

The room, though expensive by our standards, turned out to be the best room in the company. And Tom turned out to be a great roommate. We got along very well and he treated me just like a little brother. Tom was 24 and I was just about to turn 22 years old. We had many great conversations together.

Tom liked to talk about the antics of his fraternity brothers at the college he attended, St. Norbert College. He was particularly proud of the dry ice brand on his left buttock, claiming it was a brand of honor. He never talked about high school but he talked extensively about his wife Ann and his son Tommy. He would write them or send them audio cassette letter recordings regularly.

I was not that prolific of a writer. I sent and received very few letters while in Vietnam. Maybe I sent 10 or 12 letters to my family the entire tour. Fewer to Linda and Diane.

But Tom was a good example to me. He was a real professional. He liked to learn and read extensively. He always had a book with him.

1st and 2nd Flight Platoon

As the first weeks in the unit flew by Tom and I settled into our flight platoons. Captain Goodnight was right. Dennis Faucher and Dave Brammel were in my flight class. It was good to see them.

There were also others from our flight class. WO1 Larry McKean, WO1 Don Miller, and WO1 Dana Amos were also in the unit but had other assignments or were in a different flight platoon.

Brammel was still a co-pilot like me but Dennis Faucher had made aircraft commander. I was a little jealous of his status since we both had the same amount of time in Vietnam. The Air Cavalry and its focus on the ARVN pilots had restricted me. Dennis had some great aircraft commanders that mentored him and he had gotten extensive flight time. As it turned out PFC Norman was also assigned our 1st flight platoon. In fact he had received a promotion to SP4. I would fly many missions with SP4 Norman.

Tom also was getting settled into his platoon. His platoon also had some good pilots, including WO1 Bill Shillito who was the unit IP as well as 1LT Richard Trumbo, also known as "Festus." Bill was a true professional with a very smooth touch on the controls. Festus was also a good pilot. In fact he was probably one of the best seat of the pants pilots in Vietnam. It was said that he would strap that Huey to his body and become one with the bird.

But Festus was a Lieutenant with an attitude. He didn't like bullshit and he made it known. About six months prior to me coming to the 129th Festus was unfortunate enough to be struck in a mortar attack. One of the mortar rounds exploded near him and wounded him in the leg and heel of his foot. The wounds were not bad enough to send him home. So he recuperated in the unit and did not fly for a few weeks. Rumor had it that he stayed pretty drunk in the O Club.

Having acquired a slight limp from his wounds some of the pilots decided to give him a nickname from the TV series *Gunsmoke.* So they nicknamed him "Festus" and the name stuck. Unfortunately, the real character in the TV series that had the limp was "Chester". That did not matter to LT Trumbo though; he liked the name Festus and went by that name for the rest of his tour.

Self-timed portrait: Sitting on my bed in our 129th Hooch, Tom Shaw (far left), Unknown 1LT (center), Jim Crigler (right)

Chapter Twenty Six: The REAL Flying Starts

Mountain Resupply

One thing became apparent very quickly. This was NOT the Cavalry unit training ARVN pilots. This was a real combat flying unit conducting combat resupply and support missions. These guys flew all the time. The guys I graduated flight school with that flew with the 129th probably had five times the flight hours that I had accumulated thus far.

Tom and I would begin each day by reporting to the operations shack. We would grab a coffee from the mess hall before dawn and then over to the briefing room at the ops shack. There each day in grease pencil the operations officer would assign pilots to fly together and pass out known missions for the day. The known missions were usually Korean Tiger Division resupply.

The aircraft commander of the known mission was usually given a CA assignment sheet showing the unit to support, pick up and drop off LZ and a note whether the LZ was considered hot or cold regarding the enemy. The unknown missions were usually to fly to a staging area, refueling the Huey, and stand by in case the bird was needed for an operation. These missions were sometimes boring but more often than not they ended up as remote resupply, or extractions, or medevacs.

Captain Goodnight and the Matterhorn

But today I would be flying with Captain Goodnight again.

"I'm going to have you landing on some of these peaks today Mr. Crigler," he said.

Lane Army Heliport was surrounded by mountains, each with a tiny peak. Within each peak was a Korean outpost dug into the mountain by hand. These were perfect observation posts and most also contained mortar tubes to fend off the enemy or in support of friendly troops with night flares and regular mortar rounds.

The high ground held many advantages. But one of the disadvantages was resupplying these troops. This job fell to the 129th. I had not done much mountain peak landings prior to this so I was interested in getting this experience.

We started our missions with resupply of the lower bases first until we could burn off some fuel weight. Then we gradually worked our way up to the higher elevations. True to his word Captain Goodnight would demonstrate a peak landing. Then he would allow me to make the same landing (keeping his hands lightly on the controls). One little mistake on some of these landings and you could end up in a fiery heap rolling down the mountain. I did pretty well on all of the peak landings as I did not crash. But I definitely needed more practice at these landings.

"Alright Crigs, I'm going to give you your first taste of the Matterhorn," he said.

We had a few cases of K-rations, some water, ammo, and mail to drop off and the Korean RTO saved this mission for his last. Goodnight took the controls and pulled pitch. We were climbing toward the tallest peak with the smallest landing site of them all, the Matterhorn. There was a small flag on the Matterhorn outpost and you had to judge wind direction from that flag. Unfortunately the winds "swirled" and the flag usually flew in all directions.

"OK Crigs, this one is tricky. You have to just get a general view of where the wind might be coming from and then take this puppy to the ground right on top of the white "H" painted on the landing pad."

"That H doesn't look any bigger than the landing pad," I said.

"That's right Crigs and you can't really hover on this pad as the winds are too vicious. Let me take her in and you just watch," he said.

Then he started his approach. As he got closer I could feel the collective rising to slow our assent. We had slowed somewhat but I never saw a collective that high and the ship still going downward. Finally, the ship was shaking as if we would fall through. But we slowed somewhat and both skits hit the white painted H. We were inches from the side of the pad. I could see the relief of Captain Goodnight.

"Now you see why this is such a tough resupply," he said. "I'm always glad when this one's over!" Taking off can be just as bad because you could get a downdraft and it could push your tail rotor into the mountain. It's not a good day when that happens."

He asked the RTO to talk to the troops unloading and ask which way the wind was generally coming from. The Korean trooper just smiled and twirled his finger in a circle.

The RTO said, "He says wind come from all directions."

"OK," said Goodnight, "when plan A fails we go to plan B."

As soon as the supplies were unloaded we would take off straight ahead. There was a steep drop off and if we hit a downdraft we should be able to recover and get lift to fly out of there. And that's exactly what we did. Except we sort of flew down the mountainside a bit but it worked out in our favor. It was also fun flying down that mountainside.

After our debrief at the operations shack I walked up to the O Club for a burger and a beer. THIS Army O Club had cold beer. Somehow they had procured an ice machine from the Air Force.

While I was waiting for my burger WO1 Faucher walked up and said, "Say, I hear they're putting you in for the Distinguished Co-Pilot flying award!"

I looked at him quizzically.

"I hear Captain Goodnight showed you his approach to the Matterhorn today. You are a brave pilot Crigs, very brave," he said. "Most of us run the other way when Goodnight says he needs a co-pilot to fly with him to the Matterhorn. You earned your wings today." Then he said, "Say, you and I are scheduled to fly in the next week. I'll show how to do it right!"

"Looking forward to it," I said.

I knew Faucher was just kidding. Captain Goodnight was an excellent pilot. As a warrant officer it was his way of jesting with the officers above him. You were only as good as you could fly.

WO1 Crigler goofing around with Platoon Leader Captain John Goodnight

CHAPTER TWENTY SEVEN: KOREAN TIGERS

Tiger Wagon and the Korean Tiger Division

A few days later I get assigned to a regular mission called Tiger Wagon. I would be flying with a pilot that is not in our platoon, Captain Mike Hardy.

Captain Hardy is on his second Vietnam tour having flown his first tour as a warrant officer with the 129th in 1968/69. He took a direct commission to 1LT and 18 months later made captain. Now he was back flying with the 129th but in a different capacity.

He was now the Tiger Division liaison officer in charge of communications between the 129th and the Korean Tigers.

"Today we get to fly some Korean generals around Mr. Crigler. I understand from Goodnight you are one of the better co-pilots."

"I hope so Captain Hardy. Some of the warrants say I'm pretty brave to fly with him," I said.

"That's what I heard too," he said. "Well, you never know about these Tiger missions. Sometimes we just sit for hours, sometimes we fly all day. Today I'm told the general is inspecting some of the troops and we have the dubious honor of being their pilots. He requested me specifically and I requested you."

"Well thanks," I said. "Should be a learning experience."

With that we fired up the Huey and flew over to a landing pad that the crew called Tiger Town, where we shut the bird down and waited for the general. While we waited I asked many questions about the Koreans and their role in the war. Hardy explained that there were two divisions of Koreans, the Tiger Division and the White Horse Division.

The White Horse was to the south of us and supported by the 60th Assault Helicopter Company. The 129th supported the Tiger Division. He said the Koreans were some of the toughest fighting troopers in the world. He would never hesitate to support them in combat. The ARVN were another matter he said.

True to Hardy's assessment the general and two colonels arrived for inspection flights. We would visit four Korean compounds. Each time we would land then shut the Huey down to conserve fuel. Hardy and I waited in the Huey with the gunner and crew chief. We watched as the Korean general walked up and down inspecting troops. Occasionally stopping to say something to a soldier. But more often taking his swagger stick and smacking the hell out of his troops. Including the compound commanders.

"Shit, these guys are serious about spit and shine aren't they." I said.

"You're a quick learner Crigs," said Captain Hardy. "You should see them practice Taekwondo as a unit. These guys are bad asses. The VC and North Vietnamese hate fighting them."

After the fourth inspection and beating ceremony we dropped off the general and two assistants and returned to Lane for the day. It was a total of only three flight hours but pretty interesting seeing how disciplined the Korean Army is in War. This was nothing like the discipline of typical American soldiers.

Kimchi in the Morning

The next day operations assigned me to go on a couple of routine missions with 1LT Larry Lackey.

Larry was a new Aircraft Commander and these were some pretty routine supply missions. We flew in mostly lower level outposts. Definitely not like the mountain peak resupply of a few days before. These missions were north along the Bong Son River and the outpost at An Khe Pass.

This day, though for the first time, I got the distinct odor of garlic and pickled cabbage. Each time the Korean RTO came close to my face to show me the coordinates for drop off I got a big whiff of kimchi. Korean kimchi is a dish made out of cut up cabbage, radish, and scallions and seasoned with red pepper paste, garlic (lots of this), ginger, sugar and fish sauce. Believe me it's pungent!

As luck would have it at the end of the day we have a left over case of Korean K-rations. None of the crew wanted it so I took it back to my hooch for inspection and tasting. The burgers and mess hall food were getting boring so this looked interesting. I noticed kimchi in every box.

"They must eat this stuff with every meal," I said to my roommate Tom.

I pulled out a can of Kimchi and opened it up with my P38 can opener.

"Get that crap out of this room, Crigler, I have to smell that stuff all day!" Tom said.

But I took a fork and put a bunch of it in my mouth.

"Holy crap this stuff is great!" I said. I looked at Tom and said, "If you can't beat 'em, you gotta join 'em!" and with that I ate the rest of the can.

This was the beginning of a lifelong love of Korean food. For some reason, kimchi breath from an RTO never bothered me again.

Chapter Twenty Eight:
Dennis Faucher

I had talked with WO1 Dennis Faucher (pronounced "Fo Chay") many times during flight school. He was a 6 foot 3 inch tall Texan from the Fort Worth area. He was also one of the youngest pilots to graduate in our class.

He was 19 years old when he got to Vietnam. He turned 20 years old in October 1971 but was still one of the youngest pilots in our unit. And now I was his co-pilot. Frankly, I started out the day a little cocky and jealous of Dennis for getting his A/C orders so far ahead of me. And probably for the first hours flying with him I let it show. I would change my mind on this day.

"We've got some resupply up in Binh Dinh Province area, then a drop off at An Khe Pass, then some mountain missions. You have the aircraft Crigs," he said.

"Roger, I have the aircraft," I said as I flew north past Phu Cat Air Base.

Dennis took the controls to land in the bases that I had not been in before and let me get a good look around at the terrain.

It was important to get good visual comfort with your area of operation or AO.

As we approached An Khe Pass Dennis said, "I know you've landed here before but I want to show you some different approaches. This compound will be a battle ground if the NVA ever attack again as they will want to close Highway 19 right here at the top of the pass. I want to show you some alternative ways to get in here."

Dennis flew low and fast but with a precision that I had not seen from other pilots. He had what we called a "smooth touch" to the bird. He flew along the ridge just above the trees then made a hard left and descended into the Korean fire base at An Khe Pass. It was a quick approach and landing and he flew that bird like it was strapped onto his ass. I was impressed.

The Koreans unloaded their gear and once we got the all clear Dennis took off and flew low level down the right side of the pass. We came in and out of there so fast we surprised the Koreans.

"If we were under fire we would not be on the ground more than a couple seconds and sometimes you never land, you just keep hovering forward and dump the supplies and get the hell out of there," he said. "One of my first A/Cs taught me that. It may save your life Crigs."

"Norman, you enjoying this flight?" he asked SP4 Norman.

"Well, I was not expecting the low level demonstration Mr. Faucher but I'm pretty impressed sir," he said.

SP4 Torres was the crew chief on this flight and he said, "We heading back to Lane sir?"

"No Torres, Mr. Crigler and I have a date with the Matterhorn. They need some water and extra mortar flares so that will be our last mission of the day."

We had refueled at LZ English and would burn off enough fuel by the time we picked up water and mortar flares to be perfect for flying into the Matterhorn.

As we flew around the top of the mountain Dennis said, "The trick is to get the 'feel' of the wind. A tail wind will kill you and the ship will shake like crazy and you fall through. Like the crew chief of Goodnight's bird told me you guys did. But if you take it slow and a higher angle of approach, even if the winds are changing you can get in and out safely," he said.

He skillfully maneuvered the Huey at a slightly different angle than I had flown in before. He picked his target landing sight and we flew a line directly to that point. I could barely feel the skids touch the ground.

"Holy crap Dennis, that was fantastic. Nice job!" I said.

"Glad you noticed," he said. "Now you fly us back to Lane."

"No problem. But tell me, what would your takeoff area be and how would you fly it?" I asked.

Dennis told me to do the opposite of what we had done before and that there were better updrafts this time of day at a different exit point. I took his advice and sure as hell we lifted right off.

When I got back to Lane, Dennis and I shut the bird down for the day. All I could think of was how good a pilot this A/C was. He had a right to be a little cocky. I had learned more from him in one flight than any other mission. I would be his co-pilot any time he requested.

■ *WO1 Dennis Faucher (left), WO1 Jim Crigler (right), Feb 1972*

CHAPTER TWENTY NINE:
AUGIE BAILEY

An Khe Pass and Pleiku

It was now mid-March 1972. I flew with Dennis several more times that week. We flew back into An Khe Pass several times and took an American advisor supporting the ARVN at LZ English up to Pleiku near the Laos and Cambodia borders.

Dennis pointed out the graves of the French soldiers that were buried along Highway 19. Apparently a French Army command was massacred at this site by the Viet Minh (Viet Minh were the predecessors of the Viet Cong) in the mid-1950s.

"They buried them standing up and facing France," he said. "Some say that was meant to be a slap in the face to those arrogant French politicians that sent them to Vietnam in the first place."

We did a wide turn and then he flew low over the graves in a sort of Huey salute to those French soldiers, then we continued on to Pleiku. When we got there another smaller helicopter, an OH-58 Kiowa was waiting for us. A guy in civilian clothes and a white cowboy hat got out of the bird and walked over to the

American advisor who was a colonel. Our advisor saluted and walked away with the civilian.

"Who the hell is that?" I said.

"Not sure," said Dennis.

"I think that's Mr. Vann, sir," said the crew chief. "He's in charge of II Corps. We saw him on a mission last week. Wears that damned white hat. What a target."

At Pleiku was a mountain highland Army base cut out of the jungle called Camp Holloway. It was huge. It was also relatively close to the Ho Chi Minh Trail so 122mm rocket attacks were normal here.

It was also colder here, especially at night. If you did not remember your flight jacket it could be a cold evening certain times of the year. The 57th Assault Helicopter Company, the Pink Panthers, were based at Holloway. Where the 129th Bulldogs would cover An Khe Pass, Highway 19, Binh Dinh Province and along the coast, the 57th covered Kontum, Pleiku, and the Tri Border Area. Kontum was the provincial capital of II Corps and a hot target for the NVA. One ridge along the western path to Kontum was so prolific for rocket attacks that we called it "Rocket Ridge."

Corkscrew Approaches

By now I had been with the 129th for a little over one month. I had flown almost every day and had gotten more flight time than the entire time I spent with the 7/17th Cav. Both Tom and I flew extensively and we were regularly assigned to a new aircraft commander every day or so.

For me it was a great learning experience and every one of the pilots in our platoon were real pros. They all wanted to do their job and still get back home safely. They were constantly teaching me flight and combat strategies that were taught to them by previous aircraft commanders.

It was about this time that I first flew with WO1 Augie Bailey. Augie was a brash "I don't take shit from anybody" warrant officer. And he was a hell of a pilot.

I flew with Augie for a week straight and got to know him and his style of flying well. We flew all over our AO on resupply and insertion missions. Augie felt that our area of operation was getting hotter as we now took more small arms fire and the occasional bullet hit. He was ultra-cautious on certain approaches and instilled in me a cautious attitude as well.

The weather up until now had been fairly decent. But lately we had been flying in a lot of low visibility weather. This was good experience as flying around the mountains you had to keep your bearings and know your situation at all times. Many, many pilots met their fate on a mountainside crash in Vietnam. I did not want to die this way.

Mostly, we were super seat of the pants VFR pilots (Visual Flight Rules). We had no GPS or modern technology to help us if we got stuck above the clouds. Just a compass, a radio beacon, and perhaps a ground control radar operator to guide us via radio.

We were all trained in flight school on instrument flying but we did not practice it enough in Vietnam to be really proficient. Thus most of us stayed below the clouds. I remember returning on many missions flying low just below the cloud cover at 100 feet AGL (above ground level). The fortunate thing was that if you could find Highway 19 or Highway 1 you could get back to Lane by following the roads. As long as you did not run out of fuel. But at this low level you were definitely exposed to enemy ground fire.

Augie would use the inclement weather to our advantage. If there was enemy activity around a fire base, Augie would not make a direct in approach. Instead he would use the clouds as cover and fly directly over the firebase until he saw the circle of barbed concertina or razor wire. Then he would make a diving left turn in a corkscrew fashion until he was about 300 feet off the ground. He would then straighten out towards the landing pad, pull pitch, flare, and set that bird neatly on the pad each time. Three or five seconds to unload and we corkscrewed back up into the clouds again. Augie let me practice this maneuver many, many times until it was second nature. Flying with Augie Bailey and Dennis Faucher was some of the best combat training that I ever received.

I pointed my camera at Augie just as he turned to make a diving corkscrew approach into a hot LZ. You can see the razor wire out the side window. He was hollering "we're going in!"

We Drink Our Way to Sleep and USO Strip Shows

The 129th shared Lane Heliport with 498th Medevac and another Cav unit. So the O Club was a constant hive of activity. Pilots that flew all day would often drink well into the evening. And the 129th pilots were no exception.

Up until now we had not seen much rocket or mortar activity at our base. But occasionally an alarm would sound and the O Club would vacate the half inebriated pilots to the bunker just outside of the club. Then when the all clear would sound, back into the club we would go.

Around pay day there was also a lot of gambling that took place. Especially around the crap table. I was not a dice player and I had not played poker since winning the 35mm camera from the drunken captain in Saigon. But I did learn to like bridge. So did Tom Shaw. Not only were we roommates, we became excellent bridge partners. We played bridge almost nightly as we sipped our scotch well into the evening.

The exception to card playing was movie night or a USO show. The movies were usually pretty bad. Generally they were WWII movies or the occasional new release but this was rare. But we regularly had USO shows. Think cheap striptease shows. These were Vietnamese bands that would imitate U.S. bands and singers like Credence Clearwater Revival, Rolling Stones, or Elvis. And the girls would always come out and do their strip.

It was torture for a 22 year old. But we would get rowdy and have fun anyway. WO1 Bailey even had a fake WO1 complete with a human skull dressed in a WO1 Nomex flight suit. He named it Yorick after the skull of the dead court jester in the William Shakespeare play *Hamlet*.

Augie would sit in the front row with Yorick and wait until one of the strippers got close. Then he would pull a cord in the back of the skull causing the jaw to flap up and down. It would scare the hell out of the stripper and many times they would fall backwards, giving us an excellent preview of what was to come.

But all this drinking, and card playing, and talking in the bar gave us a certain level of comradery. We would gather around when the returning pilots talked about a hairy mission or what areas we were in heavy contact with the enemy. We would pass information among us.

I set my camera up with self-timer on the stage as the USO show was going on. This photo shows Yorick held by Augie Bailey and Dave Bramel to his left. You can see me peeking over Yorick's left shoulder.

Special Note regarding Yorick:
Flying low-level back to Lane Heliport, Augie Bailey noticed a skull on top of a trash heap in a field. Augie felt this skull deserved a proper burial and, as we could not leave the base, he asked his hooch maid to investigate. The next day he found a bleached skull wrapped in cloth in his room. As he contemplated what exactly to do with the skull, he felt a unique and weird connection, sort of like a lucky charm aura in the room. So he decided to give him a special place among our flight platoon until he could figure out a burial. He named him "Yorick" and gave him the most honored rank among pilots, the rank of Warrant Officer. About 6 weeks later Yorick was secretly buried at sea in a 3 ship V flight formation with Augie Bailey officiating over the prayers. Yorick had become one of us and we all wanted a proper burial for him.

Chapter Thirty: A Moral Compass

Letters from Home/Tom's Recorded Letters

Letters from home were rare for me. My mother would send me a letter or a care package every other week or two or three. But I hardly ever received letters from friends. And I remember very few letters from Linda or Diane, but when I got them I would return a note back.

It was so hard to talk about what we were doing. America was getting out of Vietnam. We were not held in high esteem and I could tell that from what I was hearing from home. It's too bad because the guys I flew with in the 129th were real live heroes.

But my roommate Tom did not care. He wanted to record this time in his life. Instead of sending letters back to his wife Ann, he bought a cassette player/recorder and a stack of blank cassette tapes from the PACEX Catalog (Pacific Exchange Catalog was a mail order service where soldiers in combat could purchase very inexpensive items like cameras and electronics). He would sit down about every other night and update an audio cassette letter to Ann.

I got to listen to much of this recording and occasionally throw in a verbal "Hi Ann" in the background. Tom would also play the recording that Ann would send back and I would hear many of these playbacks as he would listen to the return tapes multiple times. Sort of like me re-reading a letter. Ann would recount the goings on at home with young Tommy and what was going on in her world and how much she missed her husband. Her replies were so tender and warm. It made me want to survive this mess we were in.

My Confession

One day after some particularly hairy combat missions I was stressed out and skipped the O Club that night. When I walked into the room Tom was in his loft bunk listening to a cassette with Ann and Tommy in the background. It made your heart tug and it was so sweet to listen to.

Being a little lonely that day I hollered up to Tom, "You don't know how lucky you are to have that wife and kid."

"What are you talking about Crigler, you have the world by the ass!" he said back to me.

"Well, it looks that way Tom but it's not really the case. I have a moral dilemma that I have not fixed in my life and it's eating at my character and my soul," I said.

Tom turned off the cassette and leaned his head over the edge of the bunk.

"What the hell are you talking about? Of all the people I know, YOU have character. And you're a pretty good bridge player too!"

"Well, there is something in my past that I have kept to myself. It's a very big mistake and I have been struggling with what to do and what direction to take."

Tom climbed down the ladder to my bunk and sat down.

"Alright Crigs tell me about this mistake. Maybe we can help get some right direction in your personal life. It'll make you a better pilot as once you figure a plan to solve your issue it won't be hanging on your mind so much."

So I told him the whole story. At first he would give me a laugh and say "No Shit?" and then, just like Dave said to me in the days after I got my draft notice he said, "Holy crap you are fucked!"

He had never known anyone to be in this much deep doo-doo. But he listened more intently as I told the story and how I was so torn with what to do. After he listened to my whole story he was silent for a few minutes and would just say "Hmmm" every once in a while.

Finally, he looked up at me and said, "When you have a moral dilemma in your life, you need a moral compass to help find the solution. Do you love either of these girls?"

"I think I do," I responded.

"Well, then you have to do the right thing," he said.

"Alright Tom, that's the same advice I have gotten in the past. What the hell is the right thing?" I said.

"OK Crigs, let me spell it out for you: You love one of them. You need to tell her that. You need to tell her the truth. She has birthed your child. You need to be a man and ask her to marry you and take care of that kid. And with the other girl who you said you liked very much, well, you have to man up and tell her the truth as well. She has also had your child. And you have to help her raise that child as well. Look, these are two gifts from God, Jim, they're not anchors that will slow your life down. They are gifts to you to make a difference in the world. It takes courage to fly into a hot landing zone right? Well, it takes courage sometimes to right a wrong. THAT is what's called doing the right thing!"

Then he looked over at a photo of Ann and his family and said, "Look Jim, growing up I had wonderful parents that taught me certain values. And growing up in a Parochial School environment I was able to put it all together. So let me sum up my moral compass for you: There is a need to focus on what is right, not what is wrong. You need to be courageous in this life. You need to be truthful. And you need to trust in your God. The reason this is so important is that every time you run into a problem in life you will have choices. Think of it as a fork in the road. You will have to choose which way to go and which fork to take. And always remember, how you choose will form your life and those around you. A moral compass will help you. You can have my compass Jim. I know it will help you do what you need to do."

I was silent. But I was listening intently. No one had ever taken the time to mentor me in such a way about something so personal.

"Thanks Tom. That was great advice and I will take actions right away to follow your lead," I said

Then we talked about logistics and how he was planning on meeting Ann in Hawaii and he gave me several ideas on what I could do as well. Tom is a man of true character. I will remain forever grateful for his help and advice.

R & R Scheduled to Hawaii

The next day I went to the headquarters shack and put in a request for R&R (each soldier in Vietnam combat theater got seven days of rest and relaxation, call R&R. This was at the expense of Uncle Sam). Most single soldiers would take R&R to Thailand. The married guys would all go to Hawaii and meet their wives for the week.

Hawaii was important in that it was back in the States, sort of. All I had to do was call Diane, get her a ticket and fly her to meet me in Hawaii. The specialist at the HQ shack said this would probably not be an issue and gave me a tentative date of April 10th. I then went over to the other side of the base where we could attempt a MARS phone call (Military Amateur Radio Service. If the weather was right in the ionosphere you could reach anywhere in the world).

This was basically ham radio operators that would accept a communication then make a local phone call to the number you wanted by holding the microphone near the phone. The only issue was that the ham operator had to know when to click the mic on and off so you would have to say "Over" at the end of each sentence.

We quickly got a ham operator close to St. Louis. We gave him the phone number. After a few rings I could hear the phone pick up and Diane's mom answered. The ham operator asked her to accept a call from Vietnam for Diane.

"Who's it from?" she said in a slurred voice.

"Warrant Officer Jim Crigler," said the operator.

"Sorry we cannot take that call," she said, and with that she hung up.

This was more than frustrating. But I would not give up. My plan was to go to Hawaii anyway and try to call Diane when I got there. I would find someone else to make the call if necessary but somehow I would get her to Hawaii. I was going to attempt to do the right thing.

CHAPTER THIRTY ONE:

THE EASTER OFFENSIVE MARCH 30TH, 1972

Troop Strength

As we flew our missions during March we saw fewer and fewer American troops. We were now almost exclusively supporting the Korean or ARVN troops, mostly Korean.

The Americans that we did see were advisors to the Koreans or ARVN officers. U.S. troop strength was down to about 50,000 men. And only 10% of those were combat ready like us at the 129th. The other 90% were support troops and most of them were looking forward to stand down mode. Just one and a half years prior there were close to 500,000 U.S. troops in Vietnam. President Nixon was keeping his promise to pull the troops out. The rumors were flying daily about when the war would end. But the war would not end soon.

All Hell Breaks Loose

On March 30th 1972 all hell broke loose. We did not know it at the time but the North Vietnamese had quietly been massing troops for their largest invasion of the war. They sent 14 divisions of North Vietnamese regular troops to invade the south. That's over 180,000 men. And they were accompanied by hundreds of Russian T54 tanks.

We did not know these numbers at the time. All we knew was that attacks were taking place everywhere and we were taking heavy fire on almost all missions. Now we would encounter heavy 51Cal machine gun fire. This was heavy machine gun weaponry and could knock a Huey right out of the sky.

We also discovered that the NVA was now supplied with a limited number of Russian Strella heat seeking missiles. We were no longer completely safe from small arms range when flying 1500 feet above ground level. We flew all day, every day. Mostly I flew with Augie Bailey and it was not uncommon for us to get eight to 10 hours of flight time per day.

Where we would normally be tasked with flying 20 or fewer missions in a day, we were now going on 36 to 40 missions daily. And most of them we had the risk of enemy ground fire. The 498th Medevac was a busy unit as well as many casualties were being taken on our side.

A couple of days before my R&R I was called to the HQ shack. The XO (Executive officer and 2nd in command of a unit) advised me that my R&R was not approved and that according to Major Jones we could not spare any pilots, especially ones with experience.

"We need you Crigs," he said.

"Alright sir, I will put in for an R&R at a later time," I said, and with that I saluted and walked up to the Lane O Club for a beer. I would still focus on righting my wrong. But it would have to wait on the war a little longer.

Left Seat Check Ride on Combat Assault

By now I was getting to be a pretty good pilot. I had been in Vietnam for almost seven months and though the stress of combat was showing, my flying skills had improved immensely. Most of the A/Cs that I flew with were now giving me some left seat time versus the typical co-pilot right seat.

You had more visibility from the left seat but it was harder to see the instruments. You needed a better "feel" of the aircraft in the left seat and I was grateful that they let me get used to this side.

Unbeknownst to me, the A/Cs were watching what I did very closely. They would give me much more control over the missions, basically letting me run the show.

One morning I showed up at the operations shack for pilot and mission assignment.

"Hey Crigs, come over here," hollered our platoon leader Captain Goodnight. "I think you know WO1 Bill Shillito of 2nd Flt Platoon. Bill is our unit IP and he's going to fly with you today. He'll give you a left seat check ride," he said "By the way Crigs, we are hearing from the Koreans of some massive buildup around An Khe Pass. If you end up over there watch your ass!"

"Roger that sir," I said.

Then Bill and I got our mission assignments and went down to the flight line to brief the crew.

"Guys we are going on some resupply missions to some of the peaks around here and then we are on standby. But there is a lot of enemy activity around so we need to be alert and cautious," I said.

The crew chief was SP4 Robert Carazales and the Gunner as SP4 Billy South. Bill Shillito advised me that he was there as co-pilot if I needed him but otherwise he was an observer watching me conduct the missions.

"No problem Bill, happy to fly with you," I said.

We flew over to the Korean supply pickup point and loaded with the usual ammo, flares, water, and K-rations. We also picked up a Korean RTO to help us coordinate. RTO Jun was his name. I had flown with him before. Jun came close to my face and pointed to three drop off points on the map. The kimchi smell made me hungry.

The last drop off point would be the Matterhorn. "Shit," I thought, "of all the missions to get on a check ride. And to top it off I have never landed on the Matterhorn from the left seat." But I thought to myself, "Just stay cool and concentrate on the missions."

I made two easy approaches and felt pretty comfortable flying into the first two peaks. They were not that high in altitude but there was a pretty steady wind that helped. Then we went back to the supply point and loaded up for the Matterhorn. It took us a few minutes to get to altitude and about a 10 minute flight up to the Matterhorn.

As I flew past I noticed that the flag which was normally flying every which way was now flying straight out in one direction. Remembering WO1 Faucher's method of approach I flew slower than normal and a little steeper approach. I was lucky as the wind was steady and not the usual treacherous swirling that was normal for this area. You could hardly feel my skid touch the ground and we landed perfectly on the white H painted on the landing strip.

"Nice Crigs, that was almost as good as Faucher's check ride landing," said Shillito.

As we were unloading the radios started to crackle with activity.

"Bulldog 12 and Huey 526 we need you to return to Lane and refuel for rescue combat assault," said the operations officer.

"Roger, we are just leaving the Matterhorn and will be there in about 10 minutes," I said.

We flew back to Lane and topped off the fuel tanks then shut down for a quick briefing.

As the pilots gathered around, Major Jones said, "Gentlemen, we don't have long to prepare. There is a Korean company of men that is surrounded by the North Vietnamese. We're not sure how many enemy but they are estimating at least several companies and it could be as large as a battalion of NVA. If we don't get them some reinforcements and ammo they are lost. Your crews are loading up on ammo now so let's crank 'em up and go to the pickup point. Tune radios to channel 131.6. Oh I almost forgot. This is a 12 ship mission but the LZ is only big enough for one ship at a time. We have two cobra gunships on station and each troop ship will be escorted into the LZ by a Cobra. The other Cobra will stand by on station and alternate."

Then he read off a list of pilots and what Chalk number (the position in line, for example, Chalk 2 would be the second ship, Chalk 3 the third ship, etc.) each would be in the gaggle of birds.

Bill and I were Chalk 3.

"Looks like we pulled lucky Chalk 3," Bill said as I hovered into positon.

“I don’t know about that sir,” said Carazales. “Seems to me they get to target practice on the first two ships. We could be zeroed in as a target by the time we get there.”

“I think it’s going to be a shit fest for everybody and it really doesn’t matter what Chalk we are. Just stay alert on your M60s guys,” I said.

With that I took off with the flight and flew in the 12 ship formation to a staging area near one of the larger Korean compounds. We would be inserting six or seven troopers each, plus water in plastic jerry cans, and lots of M16 ammo and grenades. This would be one hell of a check ride.

CHAPTER THIRTY TWO:
WE WON'T LET THEM DIE

Air Medals and a Distinguished Flying Cross

As had become my mental custom I said the Lord's Prayer in my mind as we took off from the staging area fully loaded with troops and gear. Shillito was now reading off the gauges to help me like a normal co-pilot would do in this type of situation. But he kept his hands off the controls.

"Torque gauge in the green," he said, "and I have all radio frequencies tuned up and we are ready to go Jim."

"Roger that Bill," I said.

I did not have a good feeling about this mission. Here I was Chalk 3 in a gaggle of 12 ships that could only go into the landing zone one at a time. As we flew five miles out past the landing zone I could see the smoke from the artillery fire supporting the trapped Koreans.

They were on top of a small mountain maybe 1000 or 1500 feet above the terrain. But they were trapped in a saddle and surrounded on the high ground by NVA troops. The 155mm howitzers were blasting the hell out of tops of that saddle. I could see why these guys were in trouble. As we stayed out of the artillery line of fire we did a slow lazy S flight formation until the all clear and approach was called by the C&C ship (Command and Control Huey that will usually contain the commander controlling the mission flights).

The C&C ship would release the Chalk, Chalk 1, then 15 or 20 seconds later Chalk 2 would start his approach, then 15 seconds later Chalk 3, etc. Chalk 1 headed for the LZ and a quarter minute later Chalk 2 made the turn. As Chalk 1 was on final close approach all hell broke loose.

"Taking fire! Taking heavy fire! Breaking off left," he said.

The Cobra that was with Chalk 1 opened up with rocket and mini-gun fire on the right hill.

I looked over at Shillito and said, "Make sure you keep your hands loosely on the controls in case I'm hit."

"No sweat Jim," he said.

I felt the pit in my stomach churn and tried to control the fear that was starting to take over. I'm sure every one of the crew felt the same pit in their stomach. I took a deep breath. I only had time to think of the first two words of the Lord's Prayer. "Our Father" I thought. Then I turned in to make our approach.

Just then Chalk 2 came over the radio, "Taking fire! Heavy fire! Breaking left!"

Bill looked at me and said, "What are you going to do?" "I'm going in a lot faster on approach and I may zig zag a little," I said as I pushed the nose of the Huey over to gain speed.

Alongside me I could see Captain Lee Billingsley and WO1 Glenn Nowakowski in their Cobra fly past me to try to keep the enemy heads down.

"Good luck Crigs," I heard Nowakowski say over the radio.

I went in very fast, much faster than the first two ships and then pulled the nose back to flare the bird to slow us down as we approached the LZ. We instantly took a large number of hits on our underbelly. As I went to pull collective to slow us down and land I discovered I could not move the controls. Both gunners in the back of the ship went hot on their M60 machine guns and the troops were standing by ready to jump off. Some were on the skids.

"Bill, get on the controls, I've lost hydraulics and I can't pull up the collective."

Bill, already lightly on the controls, grabbed and we both pulled with all of our might until we pulled too hard and bled off rotor RPM.

We hit the ground hard and bounced. The shrill sound of the low RPM alarm was going off in our earpieces. Ammo, water, Korean troopers falling everywhere. But Bill and I had our hands full trying to control the bird. We were not on the ground and not in a hover but somewhere in between and definitely not in control.

"Hang in there Crigs," I heard Billingsley say over the radio as they pumped mini gun and M79 grenades into the hill top.

The smell of cordite from all the explosions was everywhere and tracers were going every which way in that LZ. Korean troopers laying prone on the ground either dead or returning fire. It was a scene from hell with men determined to kill each other. The entire episode lasted perhaps less than 20 seconds. The whole time Carazales and South stayed on those M60s laying down suppressive fire on the tree line.

It was like a slow motion movie. The ship kept moving forward uncontrollably and barely staying airborne. The whole time that shrill low rotor RPM alarm going off in our ear pieces. But we were still flying.

As we passed through the saddle LZ and came out the other side we came to a valley that opened up below us about 1000 feet. Though the controls were stiff and difficult to fly we were able to lower the collective and get some RPM back and gain airspeed. It was as if God Himself had reached down and put that bird and us in a safe position.

Finally the low RPM alarm stopped. The M60s were still going off in short bursts in the back.

"Bill can you take the controls?" I said.

"I have the aircraft," he said. "We need to get to a landing site soon before we experience total hydraulic failure."

"I'm shutting off the hydraulic switch," I said as I reached up to start the procedure we had practiced so many times in flight school.

"Let's head to Phu Cat and try a running landing over there," he said.

"Got it, let me make a radio call," I said. "Mayday, mayday! Bulldog 12 out of the LZ with heavy bullet damage and no hydraulics. We are heading to Phu Cat I repeat Phu Cat Air Base to attempt emergency hydraulics out running landing."

"Roger Bulldog 12. Any casualties on board?" came the reply back from the C&C ship.

On the internal intercom I said, "Everybody OK on board?"

"South is OK."

"I'm good sir and I think the Koreans that held on to the skids are OK too. There are two of them still on board," said Carazales.

"Got it," I said.

"This is Bulldog 12, we are green with no casualties."

"Excellent Crigs. Safe landing at Phu Cat," came the reply.

Then I pulled up Phu Cat Air Base frequency and made a call to advise them of our situation.

After we had instructions on where to conduct an emergency landing I looked at Bill and said, "You want me to do this landing or do you want to take her in?"

"Just keep your hands lightly on the controls with me in case I need help. We'll go in at about 40 knots and if we can keep the ship straight we'll be fine," he said.

I tried to keep my hands just lightly on the controls but they were shaking too much after that event.

WO1 Bill Shillito did a text book running hydraulics out landing that day. It was a miracle that we were alive. It was even more of a miracle that none of us were killed or wounded with all those bullets flying.

When the rotor blades stopped we tied off the main blades to the tail boom. Then Carazales went through the ship checking for damage. We must have taken a couple 51Cal bullets along with AK47 rounds which hit everywhere. He showed me several rotor control tubes that were shot almost completely through the tube, being held together only by the tiniest sliver of metal.

Had those tubes separated the ship would have crashed for sure as our controls would have been useless. How lucky we all were.

I reached for my camera hanging on the back of my seat armor and handed it to Carazales.

"Hey, Carazales. I want you to take a picture of me so I remember what I looked like surviving this day!"

As I leaned on Carazales's M60 machine gun the Korean RTO Jun came up and stood by me. Carazales snapped the photo. Many years later that photo would hang on my office wall. Anytime the shit hit the fan in business and the stress levels got high I would just look at that picture and remind myself that "if I could survive that day, the rest is a piece of cake."

SP4 Robert Carazales took this photo after hydraulics out crash landing

As it turned out our helicopter was the only ship to make it into the LZ that day. The few men and the ammo and water we dropped in helped to turn the tide of that battle. The Cobra gunships made a difference as well.

WO1 Bill Shillito received the Distinguished Flying Cross for that mission as the IP. The rest of us received an Air Medal with "V" device for Valor. We had all earned it.

Chapter Thirty Three:

War is Ugly

Bodies on Every Resupply

We were picked up at Phu Cat by a returning Huey and flown back to our base at Lane. Our ship would be repaired in place and flown back later in the week.

That night I did not hit the O Club. Death was close that day. I just wanted to be alone and write a few letters back home.

The next day at the operations briefing WO1 Ralph Graves was assigned to fly with me as co-pilot. I had totally forgotten about my check ride.

“I guess Shillito passed me,” I thought.

My permanent call sign was now Bulldog 12. The operations officer looked at me.

“Crigs we’ve got some resupply missions and a few troop pickups for the Koreans. Head over to Tiger Town and pick up your RTO. You’ll have a busy one today,” he said.

We cranked up the bird and flew over to the Korean pickup point and our RTO hopped on the Bird. It was RTO Jun again.

"You can't get enough of this combat stuff can you?" I said.

"It's not that sir," he said. "After you got us out of that mess yesterday, I'd fly with you anywhere."

That comment made me feel pretty good. It did not make me feel any safer.

Our job that day was to resupply outposts along the Bong Son River and the outpost at An Khe Pass. An Khe would be our first drop off and included troop replacements, mortar rounds, water, and ammo.

Lots of ammo would be supplied that day as there was much fighting the previous night.

War is ugly.

As I made the approach into An Khe Pass I saw the pile of bodies. Eight or nine in a heap and four laid out as if they were searched. One or more gave off the ugly smell of death. We landed at the pad just outside the compound and unloaded the troop replacements and supplies.

Just as the last of the boxes were unloaded I heard a "Whoomph."

I turned to my left to see another mortar round explode 30 or 40 yards to our left.

"Norman, kick that shit out the back, we're getting out of here before a mortar gets us," I said.

With that I pulled pitch and got out of there fast. We were lucky that the NVA mortar team did not have the landing pad zeroed in yet. It would not be long before they did.

The rest of the day we dodged bullets. We took a few rounds in the tail boom but no major damage. But our AO was definitely full of enemy activity.

During April we all got lots of flight time. Tom Shaw was also getting his touch back when flying the Huey now and it was just a matter of time before they would tag him for a check ride. He was thinking four to six more weeks max. He had gotten 120 hours of flight time in less than a month. I had even more than that.

That day I would count 37 grease pencil hash marks on my windshield. Just below the bullet hole above my windshield. Each hash mark stood for one combat resupply.

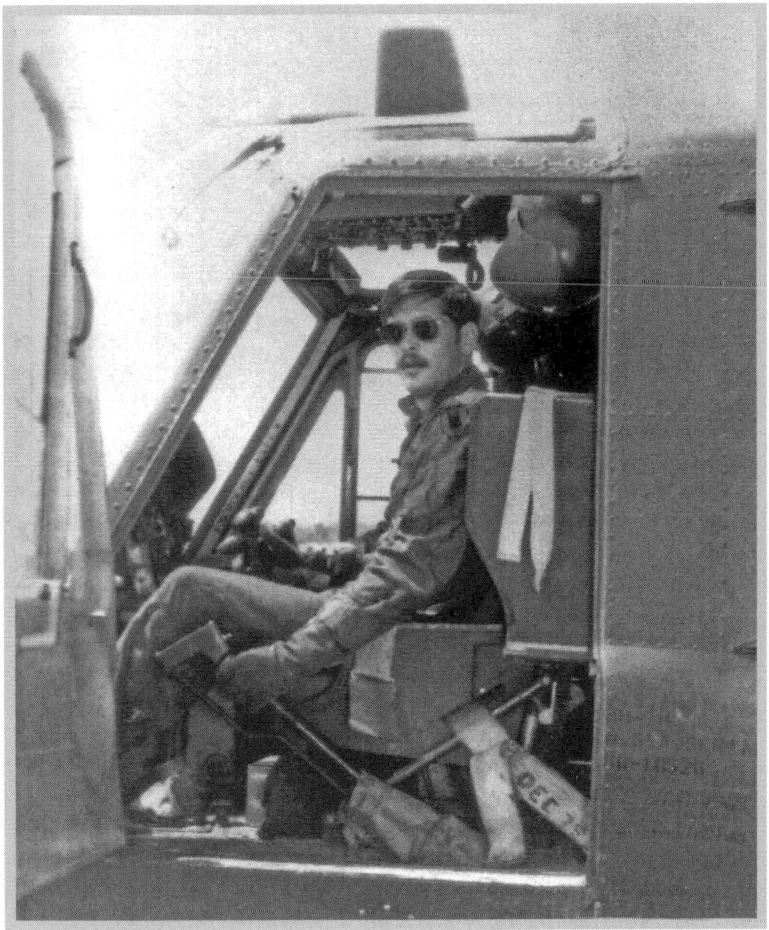

WO1 Crigler in Huey 526

CHAPTER THIRTY FOUR:

THE MEANING OF COURAGE

Pleiku & Kontum Missions

The next day I grabbed a cup of coffee as I passed the mess hall on my way to the operations shack.

As I walked through the door the ops officer immediately called out, "Crigler, we need somebody to support the 57th AHC up in Kontum. They asked for two birds for active support up near Kontum. WO1 Bailey volunteered and he thought you might want to be his wing man in the second ship."

"Sure, it can't be as bad as An Khe resupply," I said.

Augie and I cranked up our birds and flew a loose formation the one hour flight up to Pleiku.

When we landed all the ground crews were pretty spooked as they just took a 122mm rocket attack the hour before with maybe 20 rockets.

"Those rockets fucking came from every direction," said the PFC at the POL(petroleum, oil, lubricants) fueling station. We topped off our tanks and walked up to the briefing room.

The guy in the white cowboy hat was milling around with the operations lieutenant and pointing to the map. It was Mr. Vann in charge of II Corps.

"Pilots," he said looking at Augie and myself. "Are you guys from the 129th?"

"Yes sir," Augie chimed back.

"Well I'm glad you're here. I need one of you to fly me up near Dak To. The ARVN are getting the shit blown out of them and I want to assess the situation. My bird is down for maintenance and my pilot is sick," he said.

"No problem sir. My crew and I are at your service," Augie said.

"You," Van said looking in my direction.

"Yes sir?" I said.

"We need a bird for transport and resupply into Kontum and the 57th has all they can handle. Can you help?"

"Yes sir," I said.

"Good, Captain Smith here will give you instructions."

And with that Augie and I parted ways. I flew 10 or more hours that day and saw what looked like T54 tanks disabled. Vann was right. The ARVN were taking a beating. The NVA were placing their bets on beating the ARVN versus the Koreans and, even though we had seen a lot of enemy activity in our normal AO, this was five times as much. Human waves of soldiers were charging into the compounds at Kontum. The NVA had overrun Dak To and Dak To II and had significant placements on Rocket Ridge. Kontum was at risk and that is why Mr. Vann was so worried.

I got back to Lane later that night at about 9pm. It was a clear night and we could see the fighting up by Kontum and north from 20 to 30 miles away. I would not see Augie Bailey for two days.

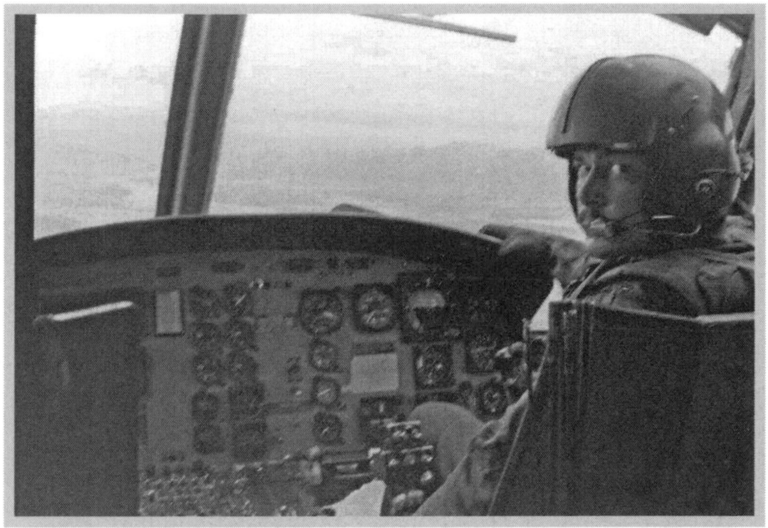

We were 10 minutes from a very hot LZ when I turned and handed my camera to the crew chief and said, "take my picture because I want to remember what I look like when I'm scared shitless". We all laughed. He took this photo.

How Can I Survive This?

The next day I was again assigned to An Khe resupply.

"Why me?" I said. "I've had this mission more than anybody else! How about some variety?!"

"Look Crigs, the Koreans like you and think you're a good pilot. That's why they keep requesting you," he said. "Besides, they know you like kimchi," he laughed.

I laughed too. I did in fact like Korean food and regularly traded my C-rations for K-rations. I would even eat in the Korean mess hall with the Tiger troops whenever possible.

But the firebases around An Khe Pass sucked to resupply. And they were getting hit hard as the NVA wanted to close Highway 19 right at the top of the pass where the Korean firebase was at. Faucher was right when he said this was the spot they would attack.

I used Dennis's ridge flying tactics and changed approach every time I flew into that base. By now though the NVA mortars were pin point accurate on the landing pad at An Khe Pass. We now had to dump supplies as we hovered at about 10 knots forward air speed, shoving supplies out the door as we moved. Mortars always fell close by. We were dancing with the devil and it was only a matter of time. And we all knew it.

The True Meaning of Courage

Back at Lane I took a nap in my hooch as I had been flying all day. Alcohol no longer helped and I was feeling the stress of flying continuously in combat. Tom woke me up about an hour later.

"Hey Crigs, let's go to the O Club and have a nightcap," he said.

"I don't think so Tom. The beer and scotch don't seem to help anymore. I've seen more dead bodies today than I ever want to see again," I said. "War is truly ugly. Today we had to transport a dead Korean soldier back to his base. He had been wrapped in a poncho liner for three days in the jungle. The smell and the maggots were so bad none of us can get the taste out of our mouths. I still want to spit.

"Mike Johnson got the worst of it. He and SP4 Norman were manning the rear M60s. We had to fly out of trim, almost flying sideways to keep the maggots and smell out of the ship. It didn't help. Johnson was puking his guts out.

"Tom, we got in so much trouble today, I swear I shit in my pants! I'm not sure I have the true courage to keep doing this!"

Tom looked at me for a minute.

"Look Jim," he said, "sometimes when the bullets are flying and you know they are aiming at you, it's scary as hell. On some of our air assaults and resupply missions my stomach churns and I feel like I have diarrhea. Being that scared and yet continuing to do our jobs over and over, well, THAT is my definition of true courage. Believe me Crigs, YOU have courage!"

And with that he reached his hand out, grabbed my arm and said, "Come on Crigs, let's go wash that taste out of your mouth.

We both walked over to the Lane O Club and downed some cold beers.

This photo was taken by a Korean soldier as we dumped supplies at An Khe Pass

Chapter Thirty Five: Intense Fighting, Intense Flying

A Very Close Call

The next day SP4 Ferrell Norman, SP4 Mike Johnson, and a co-pilot that I do not remember the name of got missions including resupply of An Khe Pass outpost.

Once again the Tiger Division had requested me. Or maybe it was RTO Jun. Regardless, we took the missions in stride.

It was a foggy day and visibility was poor. I was getting pretty good knowing the area around An Khe Pass. Several times RTO Jun took us to coordinates on the map that were wrong. In one area that we approached low we took AK47 fire and both Norman and Johnson went hot on their M60s.

The last resupply of the day was at the An Khe Pass. RTO Jun told us that the Koreans had been sending out patrols looking for the mortar tubes and that they had engaged and destroyed what they thought was the problem.

"We should have no issues with mortars today," he said.

I should have known better. On our resupply we actually landed on the helipad to unload. This firebase went through a lot of ammo and other ordnance. They were attacked more than any other base in our area. We were indeed their lifeline. As we idled on the pad the last soldier picked up a box of M16 ammo and walked at a 45 degree angle off the front of our Huey. About five or 10 yards past the blades we saw a "whoomph" that knocked him up in the air. Blood splattered on our windshield.

"Whoomph," another mortar hit and showered the ship with shrapnel. I twisted the throttle from idle and barely got up to operational RPM speed and took off bleeding RPM as I pulled collective. The low RPM alarm went on briefly, then off as we gained RPM and airspeed.

"Holy shit sir," Norman said as he looked back at the helipad, "there was a direct hit to the helipad right after we took off sir!"

RTO Jun was ashen faced as he got close to my face, "We go back now sir to main base." And with that we flew back to Tiger Town.

We had dodged a big bullet and got lucky.

As RTO Jun got off the ship he handed me a piece of brown paper and saluted me. It read:

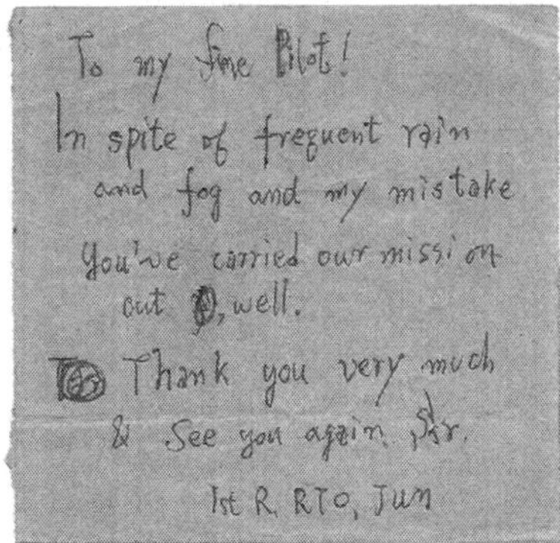

To my fine Pilot!
In spite of frequent rain
and fog and my mistake
You've carried our mission
out well.
Thank you very much
& See you again Sir.
1st R, RTO, Jun

To my fine pilot!

In spite of frequent rain
and fog and my mistake
you've carried our mission
out well.

Thank you very much
& see you again sir
1st R, RTO, Jun

I put the piece of paper in my calf pocket next to my lucky rosary. It would be my most honored Korean award of the war.

Chapter Thirty Six:

A Massive Push by the NVA

"Will you do me the honor of escorting me back to my family?"

At the end of the day I was an emotional wreck. I walked up to our hooch, opened the door and reached behind the bar for one of those bottles of bad scotch that the nameless WO1 had left us when we bought the room from him.

I grabbed a glass and poured four fingers. Then I tipped the glass and drank it all in one shot. It was bad enough to be gag worthy but after drinking a GMF I could keep anything down. I poured another four fingers.

Tom was sitting on my Air Force mattress reading a book called *Papillon.*

"What the hell happened to you today Crigs?" he said.

"I almost bought the farm Tom. I did something stupid and I knew better. I went to idle on the An Khe Pass helipad instead of doing a moving hover and supply dump. The only thing that saved us was a poor Korean soldier that got blown to smithereens by a mortar round," I said.

"Holy crap, are you lucky," he said.

"Yeah Norman and Johnson are cleaning the blood off the windows and doors and we had some shrapnel damage."

I looked over at Tom and let out something that had been on my mind.

"Tom, I have a great favor to ask you. I'm having too many close calls and the war is really intensifying. If I am killed in action my family will be devastated. Would you do me the great honor of escorting my body back to my family and comfort them if I am KIA? (Killed in action.) It would help my family immensely and it could get you out of combat for a week or two," I said.

Tom just looked at me and blinked for about ten seconds and then he said, "On one condition Crigler... And that is if I'M killed first that you agree to escort my body back!"

And with a big Tom Shaw grin he lifted up the book he was reading, waved it like a bible thumping preacher, and said, "A solemn oath my man!"

Just then the door swung open. It was 1LT Larry Lackey. He lived across the hall from us in a small one man room. As the walls were thin as paper he had heard our entire conversation.

"You guys need to cut that out and quit talking that kind of crap," he said. "I say we will all make it back alive."

I decided to have a burger and a few drinks at the O Club. Tom stayed back and read his book. Augie Bailey was at the bar and was telling me of his adventures with Mr. Vann. Dennis Faucher was there too. He had lost a crew chief flying up in Binh Dinh Province.

"Davey Stamper was a good crew chief," he said. "He was still putting out M60 fire even after he was hit. I can't help but blame myself for flying into that shit fest."

With that he downed a beer in honor of Davey. I was very glad that Augie took the mission to fly Mr. Vann instead of me. According to Augie it was a real shit fest with very high Pucker Factor flights (Pucker Factor is the slang pilots used to describe how dangerous an LZ or flight was. Pucker Factor 1 was low risk. Pucker Factor 10 you could get shot out of the sky).

As usual with Augie, I had a few more drinks than I had intended. I also felt bad for Dennis and had a few toasts with him as well. He was a real professional and a great pilot. I was certain Davey's loss was not his fault. Consequently, I got back to the hooch late. Tom was sound asleep and it did not take me long to get that way either.

A Note From Tom

I was having the most vivid dream when suddenly SP4 Norman shook me awake.

"Sir wake up! We are the last ones out and we have to head up to Pleiku, sir."

I looked up at him and then looked at my watch. Damn had I overslept!

"Oh sorry Norman, let me throw some water on my face and I'll be right down."

As Norman headed down to the flight line to prep the ship I got up and quickly got dressed. I noticed a note on the bar. It said:

Jim,
Use your courage today to focus on what is right, not wrong. Live the truth. Trust in God!
Tom

I rushed down to the armory and picked up a Car-15 with a bandolier of ammo and my 38 flight pistol and headed over to the operations briefing room. Looking at the grease board I saw my name and ship 526 listed as Pleiku. WO1 Claude Strothers and Tom were listed on resupply near Bong Son and An Khe.

I ran down to the flight line. The crew was already set and ready to crank the bird. Graves was my co-pilot today and I was happy to have him. He was one of the more seasoned co-pilots and I knew him from flight school and the CAV.

"Crank her up Ralph, I'm going to let you fly us to Pleiku," I said.

It was a cloudy day with a lot of haze.

"Take her up to 5000 feet and follow Highway 19 towards Pleiku. The clouds should hide us," I said.

"Roger that Jim."

And with that we were off to missions unknown. We would be assigned various missions once we got there.

From Augie's description last night the 57th Pink Panthers were getting the hell shot out of them.

Dak To and Dak To II firebases had been overrun by the North Vietnamese. Some of the 57th birds were lured into Dak To for supposed medevacs but it was a ruse so that the ARVN officers and some of their men could escape the firebase. When they went in they took heavy fire and as they hovered about 30 uninjured ARVN rushed the bird to get on. The crew chief had to lock and load his M16 on them or they would have taken the bird down. They barely got out of there and according to Augie took 30 bullet hits.

"It's amazing that ship still flew," he said.

The firebase was overrun not long after that.

That was where Vann wanted to go to see for himself. Vann was now using massive waves of B52 bombers to slow the enemy down so that Kontum would not be overrun as well.

We were assigned to ferry refugees out and bring supplies into Kontum. Back and forth we flew between Pleiku and Kontum all day. You could not make a straight-in approach because the enemy had surrounded Kontum. I did corkscrew approaches and take offs all day.

Throughout the day I would also see ARVN Hueys fly past us. Many of them had mopeds strapped to the skids.

"Mighty nice of them to carry the refugees' transportation," I thought.

But later as we were refueling at Camp Holloway in Pleiku our crew chief found out that the ARVN pilots were charging refugees to fly them out. The mopeds were payment. SP4 Norman was our right gunner that day.

"We should shoot those chicken shit bastards out of the sky," he said.

It was frustrating and sad to watch. But we just continued our mission.

On our last mission of the day we took some rounds through our radio panel and our main radio was dead. With that I decided to return to Lane Heliport in An Son. We were all glad to get those missions complete as Kontum was hot as hell. That day was actually worse than the missions around An Khe Pass. At least there you could hide among the ridges and fly low and fast. Kontum was surrounded by enemy soldiers and you could not fly low for risk of massive small arms fire or 51Cal fire from a tank or hidden gun position.

Oh God - Two Friends Die

We flew high altitude back to Lane as the weather had deteriorated. But we could still see the ground occasionally so I figured we could punch through a hole in the clouds after we got past some of the mountain peaks.

I flew out towards the South China Sea and when I was sure we were past the mountains I popped through a small hole in the clouds and headed towards Lane. We made a straight in approach with no radios.

When we landed I saw a private running towards our ship.

He jumped on the skid and got close to my mic and said, "Mr. Crigler?"

I nodded yes.

"Sir, the Major wants to see you ASAP sir." I gave him a thumbs up.

"Ralph you finish the shutdown. I have to head up to Major Jones's office. I hope we were not supposed to stay in Pleiku for the night," I said.

Briefing with the Company Commander

I exited the Huey and double timed up to Major Jones's office. WO1 Dennis Faucher was there too. He looked terrible.

"Sir, they told me to report right away," I said.

"They're dead Jim," said Faucher.

"Jim," said Major Jones, "WO1 Claude Strothers and 1LT Tom Shaw were both killed today at An Khe Pass."

My jaw dropped and my hands shook. The tears welled up and I could not speak.

Major Jones continued, "Crigler, I know you and Tom were close. As close as Faucher and Strothers were and I know you were all in the same flight class. After word got around the company today 1LT Lackey advised me of your and Tom's solemn oath. I want you to know that I'm sending a note up the channels to see if we can make that happen. I'm requesting authority for both of you to escort your roommates back to their families. But I can't guarantee it as we are short of pilots currently. I will update you both as soon as I hear back."

Dennis was sitting in a chair. He put his head in his hands and cried. I cried with him.

CHAPTER THIRTY SEVEN:
GOD'S HONOR ROLE

An Irish Wake Like No Other

When Dennis and I got our composure back we both headed up to our rooms. The bed was made and my spare boots were shined. The note on the bar was gone. The hooch maid must have cleaned up and thrown it away. I was an emotional wreck.

Just then Captain Goodnight and Augie Bailey and WO1 Dave Brammel walked through the door.

"We lost two great men today," said Goodnight, "and I'm not letting this day go by without toasting each of their lives."

With that he sat a bottle of Jameson whiskey down on the table.

"Where's the fucking whiskey glasses ?" he said. "Brammel, go spread the word that we are having an Irish wake in Crigler's hooch."

And so the night began.

WO1 Faucher showed up shortly thereafter and the toasts of honor began. Every officer in the unit showed up that night to toast Tom and Claude's life. And Dennis and I drank every one.

After a couple of toasts Dennis raised his glass and said, "Claude was one of my best friends and a great human being. Tom as well. They are now on the great honor roll of life. Here, here!"

We all clinked glasses.

I then raised my glass and said, "Tom was also my best friend but even more he was a mentor of my life. Here's to both of them as they are now on God's honor roll."

We all clinked glasses and downed the whiskey. I have never been so drunk in my life. I remember looking at the clock at 3am. The wake was still going on.

The next day I woke up next to Faucher. We had both passed out and were lying on the floor. My head ached. But my heart ached more. Mercifully, neither Dennis nor I had to fly that day. I slept until noon.

When I woke up I took four aspirins and prayed for the souls of my two friends. I sat in my room all day and prayed on Grandma's lucky rosary. I organized Tom's gear and personal items and made it ready to box up to send back to his wife Ann. I wondered if she knew yet.

Chapter Thirty Eight:
A Golden Star

Fond du Lac, Wisconsin April 30th, 1972

It was 6:30 in the evening and brothers David and Kevin Shaw were sitting in their living room at 161 Fourth Street in Fond du Lac, Wisconsin. The spring in this part of the state has been slow to arrive and this Sunday was still a cold and windy 35 degree day.

David who was facing the street window heard a car door slam and then saw two men exit the vehicle. He turned and looked at Kevin; his face had turned ashen white. Kevin looked out the window and saw the parish priest and a fierce looking Army officer walking up the sidewalk. Instantly they knew the reason for this visit.

The boys got their parents, Frank and Ginny Shaw, and the four of them went to the door to receive the news. But the priest and the Army officer could not tell the family what had happened as this news needed to be given to the "next of kin." They were there to speak to Tom's wife, Ann.

"Can't you please tell us what happened?" Ginny Shaw begged.

But the Army officer only repeated that they had news about Tom but could only reveal it to Ann, the "next of kin,"

It was gut-wrenching for the Shaw family. But they all got in the family car and led the priest and Army officer to Ann's parents' house where she was staying until Tom's return from duty.

The Kremer house was a short five blocks away but for the Shaw family the ride was an eternity. When they arrived Ann's mother, Mrs. Kremer, opened the door. She was so happy to see all of them arrive. It appeared that she thought they were coming over to have a pleasant evening visit.

But then she looked down the driveway and saw the priest and the Army officer. She let out a loud scream and fell back into the house on her knees. The bearers of this sad news let Ann Shaw know that Tom had been killed in Vietnam.

A dozen Catholic nuns arrived and fervently prayed their rosaries. The two families spent the rest of the night in shock and tears.

The next morning Kevin Shaw woke up at 6:00am. His first thought was "Boy that was the worst nightmare ever!" Then he heard his mother crying in the other room and he knew it was no dream. His brother Tom was dead.

Chapter Thirty Nine: Mission of Honor

A Request up to the Top Brass

The next day I was assigned to fly Tiger Wagon. This was usually a pretty easy mission as you were basically the Korean general's flight crew for the day. Most days you would wait on standby at the general's helipad. Occasionally you would fly the general or one of his colonels out to a Korean base or other event.

This day though we just waited on standby and did not fly other than back and forth to Lane heliport.

When we got back to Lane a runner came up to me and said, "Major Jones wants you to report to his office after chow."

"Got it," I said.

We shut down and I headed up to get a warm meal at the mess hall. Faucher was there so I grabbed a seat next to him.

"You get the message to meet Major Jones after chow?" he said.

"Yep, let me get this chow down and we can walk over there," I said.

When we got to Major Jones office he said, "Well gentlemen, I got permission for you two guys to escort Warrant Officer Strothers and Lieutenant Shaw back to their families. But with the shortage of pilots I had to compromise with the general so that I could get your orders approved. You will have to take this escort duty as your R&R. We tacked a couple of days on to the end of your escort orders so hopefully you can at least see your families.

"I'm sorry for this as you guys have been flying your asses off in some very difficult combat situations and you deserve a break from the action. But I figured you would both want to do the escort duty versus a normal R&R."

Dennis and I both in unison nodded our heads in agreement.

"You made the right call sir," said Dennis.

"We owe it to their families sir," I said.

The Major walked over to his desk and picked up two pieces of paper.

"Here are your orders gentlemen. These orders call for dress greens and I know you do not have any here in the combat zone. They will fit you with formal dress gear at the Oakland Army Depot. In the meantime wear jungle fatigues," he said. "Be down at the flight line at 9am. I will have a bird ready to take you to the morgue in Qui Nhon. Once there you will identify the bodies and then start the escort to Saigon and then to San Francisco. You will get further instructions at Oakland Army Depot."

Dennis and I both saluted Major Jones and returned to our hooches to get our gear ready.

Dennis and I Identify Bodies at the Morgue

Neither of us drank that night. I had not touched a drop of alcohol since the Irish wake a couple of days before. It didn't help anyway. Tom had been a good friend. Never in my life had I known someone who would mentor me and attempt to show me the right path in life. But Tom did. I would never forget it.

And now it was my turn to help him and his family. In an hour or two I would Identify Tom and start what would become for me my toughest mission of the war. My heart ached. It still aches today.

Dennis and I both showed up at the flight line at 9am. Neither of us had a clean pair of jungle fatigues as we usually wore Nomex flight suits. Mine smelled pretty bad. But not as bad as my flight suit. The hooch maids would wash them with the tiniest bit of soap. But during the day we would soak the flight suits in sweat. The hundred degree heat and stress of flying would insure that we were constantly sweating. But these fatigues were all that we had.

Both of us were nervous as LT Lackey flew us to the hospital morgue at Qui Nhon. We were met by two E5 sergeants who escorted us to into the morgue. It was cold and dank in there. One sergeant took Dennis into a side room and the other took me to another room. There on a stainless steel gurney was a black body bag with a tag on it that said "Shaw."

My hands were shaking and I was nervous as hell. The sergeant unzipped the bag and pulled it back so that I could see my friend's face.

"Is this LT Shaw?" he said.

I looked down at the naked body. Tom's face was flattened by the crash and was unrecognizable to me.

"I'm not sure," I said.

"Well does he have any other recognizable marking on his body, like a scar or something?" he said.

"Yes, he has a fraternity branding on one of the cheeks of his buttocks," I said.

The sergeant turned the body over.

"Is this it?" he said.

There on his ass was the dry ice brand that Tom was so proud of.

"That's it, I said. "I can positively identify this man as LT Thomas Shaw."

With that sergeant zipped up the bag and took me and Dennis to a waiting room.

"Sirs, you will need to wait here while we get the bodies ready and loaded into a steel casket for transport. It shouldn't take more than an hour," he said.

Dennis was clearly upset. So was I. I would never forget this day and I would always remember what my friend looked like in that bag.

The 707 Flight

When the bodies were prepared for travel the sergeant came and escorted us to a waiting truck. The coffins were already loaded and in the back of the truck. We drove to the flight line and loaded Tom and Claude into the back of a C-130 transport plane. We both saluted as the coffins were loaded. The flight to Tan So

Nhut airfield in Saigon took about an hour. We unloaded the coffins and saluted.

"They are going in that plane over there," one of the PFCs said, pointing to a Flying Tiger 707 that was sitting on the tarmac.

Dennis and I walked over and talked to the civilian pilot standing near the plane.

"Hot as hell in the country," he said.

We introduced ourselves and advised him of our mission.

"We have a lot of stuff to load up. If you want we can load the coffins up last so that they are the first thing off when we get to San Francisco," he said.

Faucher and I nodded and thanked him.

"Probably six to eight hours before we can get outta here," he said.

Dennis and I walked over to a waiting area and found a couple chairs. We would try to get some sleep. But neither of us could.

Eight hours later we were taking off in a fully loaded 707 heading for San Francisco. The plane had only one row of seats just outside of the cockpit. The rest of the plane was loaded with parts that the Army was sending back to the States for reuse. The cargo was parts, two coffins, two escort officers.

The flight was long, perhaps eighteen hours. The civilian pilots let me and Dennis sit in the jump seat directly behind the pilot. This was the FAA inspection seat but since there was no FAA personnel aboard we got the pleasure of watching these guys fly. It broke up some of the monotony of the flight.

"You guys are crazy son of a bitches to be flying those helicopters in combat," one of the pilots said.

"Yeah," said Dennis, "45,000 parts all moving in the opposite direction and made by the lowest bidder."

The civilian pilots just shook their heads.

"Well, I got to hand it to you guys, we could never do what you do," the co-pilot said.

Dennis and I went back to the row of seats in the main cabin to try and stretch out and get some sleep.

Neither of us could sleep. We ended up talking for the entire trip. I liked Dennis and respected him a lot. He was the youngest pilot in our company having just turned 20 years old in Vietnam. And I considered him the best pilot in our flight platoon. We talked about many things in life. But the elephant in the room was the Vietnam War. I told him about my brother Mike being a conscientious objector and of all the college friends I knew that were traveling "up North" to Canada, evading the draft.

I joked that I may end up in Canada myself after this escort duty. He laughed.

CHAPTER FORTY:
A COLD SLAP IN THE FACE

San Francisco Sucks

We landed in San Francisco after dark. Both Dennis and I were exhausted having not slept for days.

We got off of the plane and waited for the coffins to be unloaded. We saluted as they were loaded onto a special van sent over from Oakland Army Depot. The driver advised us that we were to catch another van that would drive us to the Army Depot.

"Wait outside of baggage claim number two," he said.

So Dennis and I headed inside the terminal and walked to the baggage area.

As we walked through the terminal we were in awe that people were just going about their business without a care. Nobody carried weapons. No one looked over their shoulders. No one seemed cautious. We had not thought about this on the flight. But we were now safe back in America. We were back in the world.

But there was something a little different that we both noticed. As we walked through the terminal in our jungle fatigues people would stare at us. Many of them giving us looks of disdain. Some shaking their head as they looked away. No one spat at us but they may as well have.

Burial Escort Training - No Crying Allowed

The looks continued until the van arrived and picked us up.

"You guys are lucky you didn't come in a couple of hours ago," the driver said. "There were war protesters all over the place earlier chanting BABY KILLERS to any returning troops."

Dennis and I just nodded.

When we got to Oakland Army Depot we were met by an older sergeant.

"You guys look terrible," he said.

"Yeah, we haven't had any sleep for days," I said.

He advised us that he would be the one training us for escort duty and that he would get us some dress greens in the morning. Then he showed each of us a room with a bed so we could rest up. I fell on the bed with my fatigues on and slept until the sergeant woke me up at 8am the next morning.

After a cup of coffee and some breakfast, Dennis and I met with our burial escort trainer. He went through the procedures that we were to use when dealing with the families.

Both of us received a neatly folded American flag.

"You are to hand this flag to the wife of the deceased at the burial site," he said. "And when handing it over you will say 'From a grateful nation.'

"Oh, and one more thing. No tears will be shed by either of you at these services. You must keep your emotional composure," he said.

From there he took us to a room filled with uniforms.

"This is what we dress the bodies in," he said "I'm sure we will have your sizes."

With that we were fitted with uniforms, name tags, award buttons, medals and rank. It was the first truly clean clothes that I had on in many months.

Chapter Forty One:
Taking Tom Home

The Flight to Fond du Lac

The next morning Dennis and I were separated.

"Good luck Jim," Dennis said.

"And to you too Dennis. I'll see you back at the 129th if I don't go to Toronto," I said.

He laughed. Both of us took a different van back to San Francisco International Airport. This time we did not have to walk through the terminal. I was relieved.

The van took us directly to a jet to load the coffin on. I saluted as the coffin was loaded. This flight would go to Chicago. From there I would transfer Tom to a commuter airline for the flight to Fond du Lac, Wisconsin, Tom's home town.

When I boarded the flight the passengers were already loaded. I got the last seat on the plane.

When we landed at O'Hare field and taxied to the terminal, the captain came over the loud speaker and advised the passengers that there was an escort officer on board and that he would be the first one off of the plane. I heard some grumbling a couple rows back. One guy saying, "This is bullshit I'm going to miss my connection."

When the plane stopped several passengers got up anyway and stood in the aisle. I got up anyway and politely walked past them, trying not to make a scene. True to his announcement the captain would let no one off the plane until I departed down the stairs to salute my friend. I could see the passengers staring at me out of the jet windows.

"This is about the Shaw Family, not about your convenience," I thought.

The next flight was much better. It was a much smaller plane but the coffin fit well in the storage compartment. I saluted. There were only about 15 people on board this flight. I sat next to an older woman who was quite talkative. She knew the Shaw family and thanked me for what I was doing.

"It was my solemn oath ma'am," I said.

"Well may God be with you on this mission and keep you safe when you return to Vietnam," she said.

The flight was short. And the passengers were much more respectful than those in Chicago. I saluted as the coffin was removed.

Ann Shaw and the Three Knocks

As the coffin was set on a gurney the funeral home hearse drove up. The driver introduced himself as the funeral director. Then the other door opened and Tom's wife Ann got out. She reached out to shake my hand.

"I'm sorry Ann," I said.

"Thank you for coming Jim," she replied.

I helped the funeral director load the coffin in the back of the vehicle. Then the three of us got into the front seat. Ann was in the middle. I did not know what words to say but I could feel the grief in the air. Ann reached over and grabbed my hand. We were both shaking. Then just before the funeral director turned the key to start the vehicle I was stunned to hear KNOCK, KNOCK, KNOCK come from inside the coffin.

Three distinct knocks.

The hair stood up on the back of my neck and Ann squeezed my hand very tight.

"That happens sometimes due to the change in air pressure during flights," the funeral director said. "Nothing to be worried about."

But Ann still held on to my hand tight. No one spoke on the drive to the funeral home. When we arrived the funeral director took us inside to discuss the arrangements for the funeral.

"Do you want an open casket for the service?" he said.

Ann looked at me.

"I do not think it would be appropriate," I said. "I'm sorry Ann but the crash left him in a pretty bad state."

She started to cry.

"I know it's hard. That's why I am here," I said. "I promised Tom that I would be here for you if this ever happened. It is hard for me to tell you this but I have personally identified Tom and after viewing him I cannot recommend an open casket funeral."

Ann just shook her head.

The funeral was scheduled for two days later. Mass would be at St Joseph's Catholic Church in Fond du Lac, WI. But the visitation at the funeral home was scheduled for tomorrow afternoon and early evening.

I went to Tom's parents, Frank and Ginny Shaw, to talk to the family and comfort them the best I could. After a couple hours with the Shaws I went back to the Holiday Inn and tried to get some rest. The only clothes I had with me were the dress greens. Fortunately the sergeant had given me two dress shirts.

Back at the hotel I was not feeling well. The time changes from Vietnam to Wisconsin and the food differences had given me a bout of stomach flu.

I called my parents for the first time. No one knew that I was back in the United States. I told them about my mission as a burial escort officer and asked if they could bring my Corvette and some extra clothing up to Fond du Lac. It was about a two hour drive from where they lived in the Chicago suburbs.

The next day I was on duty standing next to the coffin. I would take on the honor of telling anyone that would ask about Tom and his crew and the heroic actions they had made during the Easter Offensive.

I stood at parade rest for about five hours as many, many people came to pay their respects to Tom. Several of the later visitors were members of Tom's fraternity, Alpha Delta Gamma, from St Norbert's College. They asked a lot of questions.

I mentioned the dry ice brand on his buttocks and they all laughed.

"That's a brand of honor and brotherhood," they said.

Then several of them invited me to join them in a celebration of Tom's life at Odette's Bar in downtown Fond du Lac. I agreed.

The bar was lively and filled with Tom's fraternity brothers. They would do toast after toast to Tom's life. Shots of Jägermeister and whiskey and schnapps and then several would walk up to me and want to know exactly what happened.

At the time I did not know exactly how Tom and Claude had crashed but I knew the dangers of that mission very well. So I told them about the missions that he had to fly that day and what had "probably" downed the aircraft. The shots of booze and stories went well into the night. Those fraternity brothers had adopted me. They also kept me out late.

The Funeral Overflows with People

The next day I was a wreck both physically and emotionally. Too much alcohol and my stomach was still in bad shape. But this day was Tom's and his family's day. I would not shirk my duties to them.

I took four aspirin and some Pepto-Bismol. Then I took a cold shower and put on my dress green uniform.

I met the family at St Joseph's Church and we took our place at the front of the church. St Joseph's was a large church and it quickly filled up with people. At some time during the service I had to excuse myself due to my stomach issues and as I was temporarily leaving the church for a bathroom I saw that it was filled to capacity and there were hundreds of people standing outside.

Tom was well known in Fond du Lac and thousands of people were paying their respects.

When I sat back down with the Shaw Family the priest that was giving the mass, Fr. Brendan McKeough had started the eulogy. Fr McKeough was from St Norbert College and had grown up with Tom's father Frank Shaw in Fond du Lac. He gave a beautiful funeral oration entitled "The Unfinished Symphony."

As I sat back down in the pew next to Tom's parents, Frank and Ginny Shaw, I listened intently to Father McKeough. This is exactly what he said:

In 1822 a young composer was hard at work in his native city of Vienna. He was only 25 years old but already he showed remarkable talent. Still, things had not been going well for him. He was very sick; he was terribly poor; but worst of all he suffered from harsh criticism of his musical works. People seemed to like his music: the critics did not.

But he worked on, and in that year 1822 he began a symphony. He finished the first and the second parts, did some sketches of the third part, but never even began the fourth. A few years later he died, with most of his music unpublished and unknown.

Fortunately, some admirers knew and remembered that this composer had written a great deal of music that had never been made public. So for years they rummaged through his belongings and, as they suspected, discovered a treasure of music.

Among the discoveries was that old symphony written 43 years earlier. Sad to see though, it had only two movements, and symphonies were supposed to have four. But the discoverers took a long second look: these two movements were indeed fine music. No matter that there were no third and fourth movements, this was a great and beautiful symphony and is so recognized even today.

Of course you all realize, this was the famous eighth symphony of Franz Schubert, nicknamed "the Unfinished Symphony." But the musical world understood the humor of the nickname; the so-called "unfinished" was wonderfully complete. It ranked with the best. It was short, yes, but it was a masterpiece.

The Unfinished Symphony is a musical reminder of a truth that our Lord took care to tell us and show us on several occasions: It isn't how much we do or how long we do it that counts. It is, rather, how well we use what is given to us.

That is why Jesus appealed to the little people. EVERYONE was important: men and women; Jews, Gentiles, even the hated Samarians; learned and unlearned; rich and poor; sick and healthy; thieves; lepers; prostitutes; young and old. Little people and little deeds really were done away with.

However unfinished lives might seem because they were limited by position or poverty or sickness or time, Jesus offered them all a place in his Kingdom to share a happiness St. Paul found impossible to describe after a vision of it. Littleness is bigness, even greatness, as St. Theresa, the Little Flower, also reminded us not too many years ago.

In the Parable of the Talents as recorded by St. Matthew we are told the same truth in a kind of mathematical way. Exactly the same reward is promised the man with two talents as the man with five talents.

"Well done, good and faithful servant; you have shown you can be faithful in small things. I will trust you with greater. Come and join in your Master's happiness."

Tom Shaw didn't have five great measures of time: he had something more like a small two. Sort of unfinished, but still complete in so many ways. So loyal to his Church and to his schools, St. Joseph's, St. Mary's Springs, and St. Norbert's. So loving and eminently proud of the family he grew up in and of his wife and son. So true to his many friends, especially his fraternity brothers. So proud of the uniform he wore and with such distinction and the country he served doing the flying he loved so much.

All these things and all these people in his life he touched in a way filled with gusto and generosity. Tom didn't live life half-heartedly. His life looks unfinished, but there is so much more than meets the eye. We may call it a brief life, but certainly not an incomplete one.

No - this morning we celebrate a winner, not a loser. Someone who was so very faithful in the use of his two measures of time; someone already joined in the Master's happiness.

For us now it is important to remember the Master's happiness, which is the resurrection, and to await it with patience. Recall the story of the two disciples on the way to Emmaus shortly after the resurrection. How disappointed they were in Jesus' short life until he showed Himself and reminded them of His glory and His new resurrected life.

"We are a resurrected people," says St. Augustine, "and our song is Alleluia."

Recall also how sad the apostles were at Jesus' talk about leaving them - as St. John tells it in the beautiful Last Supper discourse. But Jesus tells them it is "only for a little while. Then I will see you again and your heart will rejoice; and your joy no man shall take from you."

These must be our thoughts too. Surely we shall miss Tom Shaw, miss him sorely. But his "unfinished life" is already a new and marvelously complete and happy life. For a little while we shall not see him, but then again in a surprisingly little while, we shall see him. And that joy no one - NO ONE - can take from us.

And with that Father McKeough finished the eulogy and continued the mass to its completion. There wasn't a dry eye in that church except for mine. It was my duty to honor Tom and remain stoic. Those were my orders. But it was all I could do to hold back the emotions.

A Flag From a Grateful Nation

The pall bearers took the coffin down the aisle to the funeral hearse. From there we had a procession of cars to the cemetery. The line of cars had to be five miles long.

As Father McKeough said the prayer of burial and lowered Tom's casket into the ground, I stood at my best military attention and handed the neatly folded American flag to Ann Shaw.

"From a grateful nation, Ann. We honor your sacrifice," I said.

Ann took the flag and quietly cried.

After standing at the gravesite for what seemed like hours we left and returned to Frank and Ginny Shaw's house. Some neighbors and a few nuns had prepared a meal. The Shaw family was so gracious to me. My heart ached for these wonderful Americans. Frank and Ginny seemed genuinely concerned about my welfare, especially my return to combat in Vietnam.

After several hours they took me back to my hotel. I was exhausted and collapsed into the bed and did not wake up until a phone call at about 8am the next morning. It was Ginny Shaw. She invited me to share brunch at their home this morning and also wanted to tell me that my mom and dad had brought up my car and a change of clothes.

"Thank you," I said. "Are my parents still at your house?"

Ginny advised me that my parents did not want to disturb me and immediately returned to the Chicago area. I thought this was strange indeed.

CHAPTER FORTY TWO:

THE CORVETTE WEEPING

A Trip to St. Louis

I took a cab to the Shaw home and joined them for a wonderful late breakfast. My blue Corvette was parked out in front of the home. After brunch we chatted about the war. Frank had saved a *Milwaukee Journal* newspaper that he had read the day before being notified of Tom's death. On the front page was a picture of a crashed helicopter and the headline "Dangerous missions for U.S. helicopter pilots."

The photo was of Tom and Claude's Huey that had crashed into the hillside.

"How ironic that this was in the news even before we were notified," Frank said.

I agreed.

Major Jones was on standby with the C&C ship at the time of Tom and Claude's crash. With him was a famous reporter, Peter Arnett and a photographer named Horst Faas, one of the most famous photojournalists of the Vietnam War.

They flew to the crash site within ten minutes of the crash. When they got to the site it was already secured by Korean troopers. Peter wrote the story later that day and the photographer took several detailed photos and wired them back to Associated Press.

The photos and the story were carried nationwide by many newspapers, including the *Milwaukee Journal*. The speed of our American press had beaten the bureaucracy of the military death notification system by two or three days.

Then the conversation turned to me.

"What is next for you Jim? Where will you go now?" Ginny said.

I advised them of my plan to go to St. Louis and ask a girl to marry me. I told them of the help Tom had given me and that I was going to take his advice.

"I have three days of leave left and I think I can get to St. Louis in seven or eight hours. Then it will take me two days to get back to my unit in Vietnam," I said

"Well you'd better get going then," Frank said.

And with that hugs and handshakes were exchanged and I went out to my car to leave. But when I got in my car I could not leave. I just sat there, an emotional wreck. With my official mission complete I was now overwhelmed with grief. I must have cried on my steering wheel for ten minutes before Ginny Shaw came out to my car.

She lightly tapped on my window as she could clearly see I was crying away.

I rolled the window down and she kneeled down and said, "It's OK Jim. You carried out your duty well and we are forever grateful for what you have done. We will all pray for you son and hope for your safety in Vietnam"

She leaned in and kissed me on the cheek.

"Thank you Jim. God speed," she said.

"Thank you Ginny," I said.

Then I started my car. As I drove away I couldn't help but think of that wonderful family and mourn their loss.

Photo that appeared on front page of the Milwaukee Journal courtesy of Horst Faas/Associated Press

Chapter Forty Three: It's a Long Drive to St. Louis

I Can't Believe People are not Carrying Weapons

I had 45 dollars to my name. As I stopped to fill my gas tank up I was amazed at how nonchalant everyone was about the war. It was as if we were not at war. As if no one cared what was going on in Vietnam. I was in shock at this attitude. I thought, "We are at WAR, people!"

Car Breakdown

I was now on a mission to get to St. Louis. I bypassed my parents' house in Park Ridge, Illinois and headed straight down Highway 55 towards St. Louis. But about 100 miles south of Chicago I ran into problems.

My left rear wheel was wobbling like it was about to fall off and it was making a terrible screeching noise. I pulled over into the small town of Chenoa, Illinois and pulled into a gas station auto repair shop that was closed. As I sat there frustrated and pondering my situation an old pickup truck drove up.

The big old guy behind the wheel rolled down his window and said, "You got problems sonny?"

I shut my car off and got out to talk to him. It turned out that he owned the auto repair shop but could not get parts until the next day. I told him of my escort duty and my mission to St. Louis and how much time I had left before I had to return to Vietnam.

"No problem son, I'll have your car repaired for you tomorrow. Probably just a wheel bearing," he said. "The Greyhound bus will be at the station in about 20 minutes and it goes through to St. Louis."

Determined to get to St. Louis I got on that Greyhound bus and five hours later I was in the downtown St. Louis bus terminal. It was early evening at about 8pm.

A Drunken Mom and no Diane

I put a quarter in the pay phone and dialed the number. Diane's mom picked up the phone.

"Mrs. Pastors, please don't hang up. It's Jim Crigler and I –"

"Click."

She hung up the phone. My heart sank.

I Must Tell Linda the Truth

I decided that I at least had to fix some of my situation. Even if I could not see Diane, I would try to see Linda and talk to her about everything.

I called Linda and she was overjoyed to hear from me. I had not had time to call anyone but my parents and let them know I was back in the States.

She would grab a friend with a car and come down to the station to pick me up. It was good to see her and she was very happy to see me alive. We talked the night away with her girlfriend present. I said nothing of Diane and my other child.

The next day Linda's girlfriend gave us a ride back to the bus station and we both hopped on a Greyhound bus headed back north to Chenoa, IL. I figured I would have plenty of opportunity to talk to her on the bus or on the ride back to St. Louis. I was wrong. The bus was crowded and you could hear all of the conversations. This was no place for an intimate discussion.

A Kind Mechanic

When we got to Chenoa, IL the mechanic was waiting.

"Got 'er fixed for you son. As I thought, it was a wheel bearing. Kind of surprising since you don't have even 5000 miles on that car," he said.

When I asked him how much I owed him for the repairs he refused to take any payment.

"You got it tough enough going back to Vietnam," he said. "This one is on me!"

It was one of the kindest acts to happen on my leave and one that I never forgot. I only wish I had remembered his name.

I drove Linda back to St. Louis as I would have to immediately turn around and head back to Chicago.

My flight to San Francisco would leave at 3pm the next day and my orders returning said I had to be at my unit the day after that.

I don't know why I did not bring up Diane with Linda on that car ride. I meant to tell her the whole story. She deserved that.

But sitting there talking to her, well, the words of truth just failed me. It was easier flying into a hail of bullets than mustering the courage to tell that sweet little girl that I had another love. And I wasn't even sure that I had another love anyway as I had not talked to or heard from Diane in many months.

The truth had failed me. I just could not bring myself to hurt that girl's feelings. She didn't deserve that either. I thought about Tom Shaw. Following a moral compass is not always easy.

A Meeting With My Dad

I dropped Linda off at her apartment and said my goodbyes. Then drove the five hours north back to my parents' house in Park Ridge, IL.

My parents were waiting to talk to me. They were upset and scared to have me return to Vietnam. Though Mike had safely returned from Vietnam they had read in the newspaper and seen on television much of the new offensive that the North Vietnamese were pushing and they knew I was at extreme risk. Their fear was so great that they could not face me in Fond du Lac as I buried my friend. That is why they just dropped my car off without a word.

This was the first time in my life that I saw a true concern for me from my dad. He had not written me once while I was in the service or in Vietnam. But now he looked upon his son for what he feared might be the last time he would see him alive.

The next day my dad drove me to O'Hare Airport for my return flight. I could tell he wanted to say something to me but the words never came. When he dropped me off at the departure area I got out and waved him farewell.

My dad got out of the car and stood by the car door.

"Jim," he hollered, "I love you. Be safe."

I could see the tears in his eyes.

"See you in September Dad," I said.

Then it was into the mass of people getting airline tickets. It was the first time that I remember my dad ever telling me he loved me.

Chapter Forty Four:
Non-Stop Flying

Return Flight to Vietnam

I was wearing civilian clothes on the return flight and planned on changing into my jungle fatigues before landing in Vietnam. The stares of disgust from the passengers in the terminals weren't as bad as before. But it was still easy to pick out a serviceman due to the short hair. Almost every civilian male had longer hair in 1972.

I had a United Airlines flight to San Francisco International and from there I was to catch a Flying Tigers 707 back to Vietnam.

I was glad to have the escort mission complete. But I was also nervous about returning to Vietnam. I was mentally tired and emotionally I was totally drained.

The Flying Tiger flight ended up having engine problems and we made an unscheduled landing in Yakota, Japan. The crew and I were not allowed to leave the plane while the repairs took place so I mostly slept.

Thirteen hours later we would take off for Saigon. I was now a day late getting back to the 129th. When I finally arrived at 6pm that evening I found Dennis Faucher in the O Club pondering whether I would indeed return or end up in Canada.

"We thought you went to Toronto," he said.

"No, but it was a tough mission to Fond du Lac," I said.

"Yeah, me too. I almost got into a fight at Dallas Airport," Dennis chimed in.

May 1972

At 5am the next morning I was cranking up Huey 526 for a full day of missions ahead.

It was about the 15th of May and the Easter Offensive was in full swing. All of the pilots were briefed on the B-52 bombing runs and where we needed to stay clear of when flying. Most of these bombing runs were near Kontum but occasionally they were in our regular AO.

We also now had much better reports on enemy activity and there was a lot of it. There were no safe firebases to land at and extreme caution was advised on all takeoffs and landings.

"Wear your chicken plate," (the Army's version of personal chest armor - it wouldn't stop a bullet straight on but if it hit at an angle it would deflect the round) the operations officer said before I left for the flight line.

I remembered what Augie Bailey had told me.

"The terms 'protective armor' and 'helicopter' are mutually exclusive," he'd say. "If you are wearing body armor, the bullets will probably miss that part!"

But we wore body armor anyway. Any protection from the front was OK with me as bullets had little trouble penetrating the chin bubble and Plexiglas windshield. Mostly, we were sitting ducks from the front of the aircraft.

Resupply, Resupply, Resupply

1LT Larry Lackey from across the hall moved in to be my roommate. It was a real relief to me as I could not sleep in that room alone.

With Larry snoring away I was finally able to get some real sleep. Larry was happy because he finally had air conditioning and a place to hide when the XO came looking for RLOs to pull escort duty on the roads to Qui Nhon. He, like me, did not like that duty. He was a pilot.

For the next three or four months every pilot would max out his flight time monthly.

We were not allowed to fly more than a 145 combat flight hours in any one month. And we would hit that pretty quickly.

It was great to get a couple of well-earned days off after flying in combat non-stop for weeks at a time. Mostly on our down time we played cards. Typically it was a bridge game and the pilots got quite good at this game.

But the resupply had to continue as the war was expending lots of supplies, especially ammunition. And there were always troopers to haul.

I'm sure there were months that I flew close to 200 hours but operations just did not report it. Either that or the hours would go on the ops officer's time card.

Almost all of the pilots and crew earned medals for bravery during this time frame. And a few were even awarded. But in the reality of this war, most of their bravery went unrecorded. None of us cared at all about medals anyway. Medals are OK, but having your body and all of your friends in one piece at the end of the day was better than any medal.

In late June I got a letter from my mom. She had sent a news clipping of a photograph of a young naked Vietnamese girl running away from a Napalm attack.

The article was dated June 8th, 1972 and it turned out to be the famous photo of children including the naked nine year old Kim Phuc running away from a Napalm attack on suspected Viet Cong hide outs.

I was appalled at the article as it made it appear that the U.S. troops were at fault. In reality it was the ARVN Air Force planes that dropped that Napalm.

Shot Down from a Hover

There were many close calls during these months. Once while on approach to what we thought was a relatively safe firebase, we took a bullet in the engine housing.

Loud sudden noises in a helicopter WILL get your undivided attention.

As we unloaded I checked the gauges while the crew chief and gunner looked at the ship for telltale bullet holes. They saw none. Instruments all looked good.

As I picked up to hover for takeoff the engine suddenly lost RPM and died of fuel starvation. I set the bird down in place. It turned out that a fuel line was severed by a bullet that had entered in an area hidden from view. That's why the chief did not see the hole.

We tied the bird down, pulled off our M60 machine guns and headed into the bunker compound. The crew chief found the bullet hole and the problem fuel line pretty quickly.

We radioed for a spare fuel line and in two hours we were back in business. But had I taken off just 20 seconds prior with that busted fuel line the story would have had a much different ending. We got lucky.

CHAPTER FORTY FIVE:

DEATH IS ALWAYS CLOSE BY

We Kill a Kid Who Tries to Kill Us

It was July 1972 and by then the North Vietnamese spring offensive was starting to slow down.

I had been on hundreds of intense combat insertions, mostly around the mountains near An Khe, the jungle surrounding Pleiku, and the battles for the provincial capital of Kontum.

I became numb as the days wore on. We would fly out at dawn to a staging area, shut the bird down and wait until we were called by our Command and Control ship for various missions.

Sometimes they were routine re-supply missions, but most times you never knew. The boredom and waiting, sitting in the heat of the jungle was disgusting. I just mostly chain smoked cigarettes.

Around mid-July we were supporting a clean-up action with the Korean Tiger division. Our job was to insert troopers into various LZs where they would fan out to find the NVA troops, which had gone silent on us for a few days.

I was assigned to several landing zones that were thought to be pretty safe and insert a team of seven Koreans at a time. The LZ was searched the previous day and prepped hard by the Cobra gunships prior to insertion so it was reported to us (assumed) that there was no enemy around.

I inserted the first group of Koreans and went back to the staging area for another seven troopers to insert. The first group had fanned out to form a perimeter and waited for our return. On my second approach we were informed that the LZ was still cold and no enemy fire had been taken.

As we landed in the grass to off load the troops all hell broke loose. We seemed to be taking fire from 360 degrees. M60 machine guns from the gunner and crew chief on both sides going hot but no one could see the enemy shooting at us from their concealed positions.

As the troops were getting off and running towards the perimeter I looked at a grassy area off of the nose of our Huey about 15 to 20 yards in front of me and saw what looked like a 10 year old kid in black shorts and a pith helmet.

I suddenly realized that this kid had an RPG (rocket propelled grenade) launcher and was aiming it right at ME! I pressed the intercom and screamed to the gunners to nail this kid but the M60s could not shoot directly in front of the helicopter due to the stop mechanism put on the gun turret to keep gunners from shooting their own ship down.

The kid was pulling the trigger hard but nothing was happening. I was so close to him, I'm sure he could see the panic in my eyes. And I could see panic in his eyes as well. If he got that RPG off and hit us we were all toast, crispy critters, and blown to smithereens.

I did not wait for the all clear of troops off in the back but instead pulled collective, gave left pedal (to rise the ship in the air and turn sideways) and screamed for my gunner SPC4 Norman to "Get that kid!"

As I turned left the kid finally figured out what was wrong and fired the RPG. It went directly under the skids of the Huey, missing us by mere inches. As the baby NVA trooper fired so did Norman with his M60. We were never so lucky. The kid was literally cut in half by M60 rounds. I pulled pitch and got the hell out of there as fast as that ship would take us.

I made several more insertions into that LZ that same day. It turned out to be a small force of NVA. The Koreans kicked their butts.

But as I flew in and out of that LZ during the day I could see the body of that kid laying there in the sun. The boy was literally ripped in two and held together by parts unknown. Blood, intestines, and other pieces... just lying there. Black shorts and sandals and blood. And those eyes.

Since the landing zone was small I had to land in the same spot for every flight return. The kid, just lying there with his eyes open. Dead. He could not have been more than 10 or 12 years old. There he was, just a dead stare. We lived and he had died. A failed safety, or perhaps in his terror he forgot to take the safety mechanism off prior to firing the rocket propelled grenade. But in a matter of seconds my panicked flight maneuver and his mistake saved our lives.

I looked back during one of our landings when the kid's body was lying just outside of Norman's side of the Huey. I could see tears running down Norman's cheeks. We had all been so close to death, seconds in fact.

We hardly spoke, with the exception of the gunner and crew chief saying "clear right", "clear left sir" prior to maneuver for takeoff.

None of us ever spoke about that RPG under the skids. It would have been a great drunken story to tell at the O Club but perhaps it was superstition or perhaps we were just so mentally impacted by the event. None of us ever mentioned it.

But for me, I was never the same after that day. Even in Vietnam, but maybe thousands of times since then, I have awoken holding my hands out to block the RPG hollering, "Norman!"

I can still see the eyes of that kid, panicked, trying to kill us all.

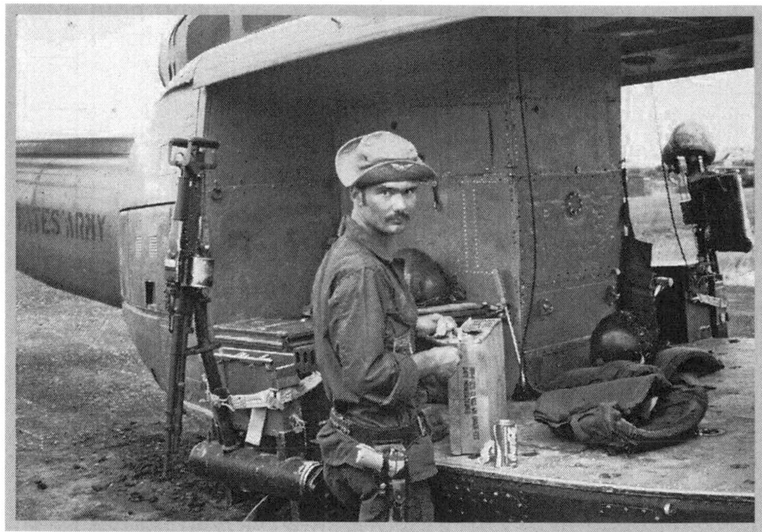

Ferrell Montana Norman SP4 Gunner

Billingsley and Nowakowski Die

The North Vietnamese were getting increasingly more sophisticated weaponry. We had heard reports of aircraft being shot down by heat seeking missiles. These were developed by the Russians and were called Strella Missiles.

All units flying in Vietnam were now sent new replacement exhaust cowlings that directed the exhaust heat up into the rotating blades to dissipate the heat signature. This did little to help and we reverted to flying low just above the treetops and fast. This protected us from the missiles but we were now exposed to more small arms fire.

On July 22nd Captain Lee Billingsley and WO1 Glenn Nowakowski were flying Cobra combat support in the jungle highlands between Pleiku and Kontum. Rumor had it that their tail boom was exploded off by one of those rockets. Lee and Glenn didn't stand a chance as their Cobra corkscrewed down to earth.

1LT Larry Lackey and crew. Notice the exhaust cowling changes.

These two gunship pilots were well liked by the Huey crews. They would often cover us with suppressive fire as we went into hot landing zones. They knew us all by call sign and would encourage us as we flew into those hell holes.

I particularly liked Lee and Glenn as we became close after my combat assault check ride. Glenn could not believe that Shillito and I did not crash that Huey after bouncing so hard. But now two more of us were gone. And another Irish wake. I will never forget their bravery and comradery.

Chapter Forty Six: Who Gives a Damn?

A Give a Shit Attitude

By now my attitude was starting to suffer. After the trip back to the States for burial escort duty and seeing the horrible support that we were getting from the American public I made up my mind that I did not want to die for this cause.

It was now August 1972 and I had fewer than two months left in my Vietnam tour. I would be cautious. I would do my job but I tried to take no unnecessary missions.

I also finally got a letter from Diane. She advised me that her parents had kicked her out of the house back in May and that she and Lisa had moved into an apartment. I was livid. Her mother could have told me that when I called her from the bus depot.

But I calmed down and wrote her back right away and asked if I could meet her when I got back to the States in September. I now had her address and was able to write with no interference from her alcoholic mother.

Fly Hard, Drink Harder

We continued to get extensive combat flight time. According to the Army we would receive one Air Medal for each 25 hours of combat assault time or for each 50 hours of flight time in Vietnam.

As pilots we never understood the difference between the two since we were shot at ALL the time on almost all missions. We were becoming some of the best pilots in the world. Even our lowest flight time pilots had more combat flight time than the highest Aces of World War II.

I had learned a lot from my fellow pilots and like them I was maturing and becoming a real man in that Huey helicopter. We all seemed to grow into men under those rotor blades.

Bill Shillito, Augie Bailey, Dennis Faucher, Larry Lackey, Captain John Goodnight, and all the rest. It was an honor to fly with them.

But I had learned much in my year with these men. I learned that above all else, we were fighting and flying for each other. I learned that we could push ourselves to the limit, physically and emotionally. And then push ourselves even more. I learned that at 22 years old I had developed an uncommon ability to watch a friend die, gather his things up to send to his wife, and go back to the flight line and fly another day. I learned that you needed some sort of compass in life, and I learned through my friend Tom Shaw that it was OK to share that compass.

But as our tour and the war lingered on all of this took a toll on each of us. For most of us, the O Club was our respite. The Lane Army Officers Club. There we would self-medicate and try to erase the bad parts of our day and think of home.

I Take Up Photography

As the days wore on and my time left in Vietnam got shorter I tried anything to keep my mind off the dangers that we faced each day.

I met a sergeant at the mess hall that turned out to be a military combat photographer. He actually had a dark room and film processing and printing facility very near the Lane O Club. He invited me to watch him on one of the down days when I had maxed out my flight time and had nothing to do.

"It would be more productive than drinking all day," he said.

He was right. I instantly took more of an interest in this hobby. The sergeant would supply me with black and white film. I would go on various missions and take hundreds of photographs. Then, later when I had time he would mentor me on developing the film and printing photos. I took many hundreds of photos during these days.

Just Pull the Damned Tooth

But I also had other issues to deal with. In particular I had a tooth that was giving me problems.

A molar in the back of my mouth was hurting terribly. It made me brush my teeth better but that did not help the already bad molar.

I went to the dentist in Qui Nhon the next day.

"You will have to wait until next week when the regular dentist come up," the Doc said. "You need a root canal."

"I can't wait Doc! I'm in too much pain, just pull the damned tooth!" I said.

The young dentist looked at me and said, "No problem."

10 minutes later the new dentist was showing me my tooth that had just been extracted.

"Too bad, we could have saved this one. But I understand the pain. Take some aspirin and NO FLYING for two days. You're medically grounded," he said.

I did not say anything to the pilots about not flying (due to a pulled tooth) as we flew on our way back to Lane Heliport. I did not want to take a deuce and a half the 20 mile ride back to my hooch.

But two extra days of no flying was definitely a bonus. I never regretted pulling that tooth. It may have saved my life.

Rocket Attack - "Dinks in the Wire"

I settled in for two medical no-fly down days. I had saved the last book that Tom Shaw was reading just before he died. Tom told me he enjoyed the book and recommended I read it after he finished.

Papillion was the name of the book and I would dive into reading it.

That night I sat in the O Club having a scotch and water and listening to Augie Bailey and Festus talk about the actions of the day. Suddenly the alarms went off.

"Everybody get in the bunker, we're under attack!" one of the officers yelled.

Not to waste any good booze the three of us grabbed our drinks and ran to the bunker just outside of the O Club.

We heard no rockets or mortars. But there was a Cobra gunship flying. For the first time I got to see what the troops see when those Cobras go hot when you are on the ground.

Captain Billingsley's replacement was a warrant officer named Ron Paye and Ron had night gunship duty this night. He had cranked that Cobra and he and his co-pilot were flying in a matter of minutes.

As Ron flew directly above the O Club he let loose with a pair of 2.75 inch rockets directly into the wire.

"Swish kaboom!" went those rockets as they exploded with the ground shaking around us.

We all high fived, oblivious to the possible dangers and sipped our drinks. We had been at war so long none of us even acted afraid.

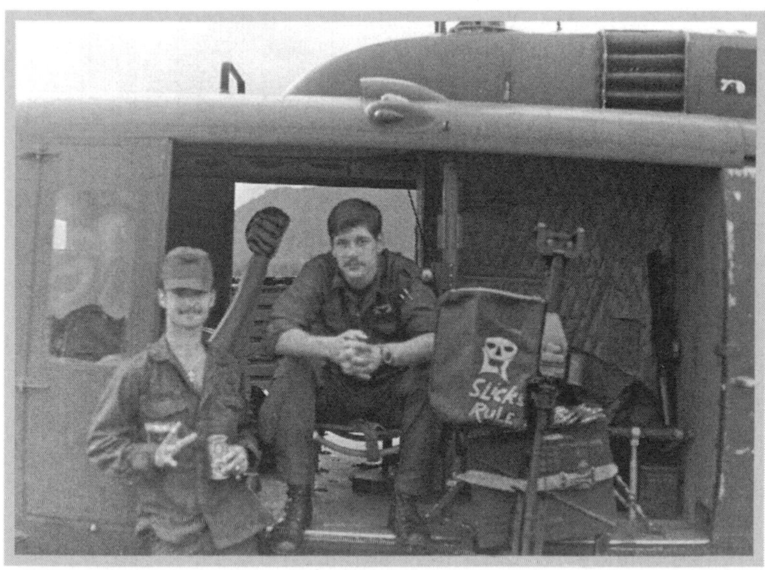

SP4 Norman and WO1 Crigler on Tiger Wagon.

WO1 Paye fired a few more rocket pairs and then flew higher to remain in stand-by mode while the ground troops inspected the area.

It turned out to be a prostitute trying to get onto the base through the wire. I was not surprised that there was not a big force of NVA attacking. We all had total faith in the Korean Tiger division that protected our surrounding terrain. The Koreans were some of the best and toughest combat soldiers in the world and the NVA had great fear of them.

The prostitute in the wire was wounded but survived. The rest of us went back to the O Club. We would later give Warrant Officer Paye a lot of verbal abuse for protecting us from that dangerous prostitution combat assault. He had kept us safe.

CHAPTER FORTY SEVEN: THE WAR CONTINUES

Combat Flying

Two days later I was on missions again. There were several small three ship combat assaults north of Lane in Binh Dinh Province. We would be inserting Korean troops that were searching for NVA positions in that area.

Ron Paye would accompany us on many of these missions and cover us very similar to the way that Captain Billingsley and WO1 Nowakowski would on these hot missions.

He would fly in and prep the LZ as we flew behind in one of the three birds as Chalk 1, Chalk 2 or Chalk 3.

"She's all yours Crigs," Paye would say as we did a quick three second land and take off.

I liked the gunship pilots that talked to us on the missions. The ones that used our nicknames, like "Crigs" instead of our more formal call signs like my "Bulldog 12."

Like Billingsley, Ron Paye was a hell of a pilot. And as a gunship pilot you needed a lot of guts to go in first with guns ablazing. Ron Paye had balls of steel. Although the gun platoon stayed generally to themselves, many of us would make it a point to buy Ron Paye a drink at the O Club.

There was no such thing as a fair fight in war. You either win or lose. With pilots like Ron Paye you win.

But the missions continued. Day in and day out we flew. I became numb emotionally and just did my job as best I could. As a short timer with less than a month to go I was mercifully assigned to some of the less risky, at least combat risky, flight missions.

But there were still the occasional body transfers for the Koreans. These were usually men that were killed in the bush and could not be gotten out right away. As most fighting units do not carry body bags these dead soldiers were simply wrapped in ponchos and carried out to a pick up site when the fighting was over.

A human body will deteriorate very quickly in a steaming jungle and after a few days the blow fly eggs turn to maggots and the body is ravaged by nature. The smell is one that you will never forget for the rest of your life. Sometimes the body fluids would ooze out and onto the floor of the main cargo compartment.

We would always have to find an area to wash the cargo bay out and flush with water before we could continue missions. Many a pilot and crew member would gag and throw up on these missions. But they were necessary as the Koreans, like the U.S. soldiers left no one behind. This was after all someone's son or father or husband that we were returning.

I earned a deep respect for the Korean soldiers during this time. They were incredibly disciplined and held to a much higher standard than the U.S. soldiers. Several times while on Tiger Wagon we flew the Korean brass out to various field units.

If the battle was going well the unit commanders were complimented. If the battle was not going well we often times saw officers beaten with a swagger stick right in front of their men. This shocked me at first until the RTO would advise that this was the "Korean way" and the commanders and men expected it.

I hauled many Koreans into and out of combat during my time with the 129th Bulldogs. Once we picked up a Korean soldier that was holding his foot in his hands. He was loaded on our ship and we took off to drop him off at the hospital in Qui Nhon. He never flinched, never cried, just a stoic look on his face. These were tough war fighters and I would for the rest of my life respect and admire the Koreans for being such great allies to us during the war.

The ARVN were a different story. Perhaps they were too tired of their war. Or perhaps it was the forced conscription of young men into the military. It was as political, maybe even more so, than the situation in the United States.

Buddhist monks would pour gasoline on themselves until they were soaked. Then lighting a match they would make the ultimate statement to end this awful war. Because of all this, and much more, the ARVN were not an effective fighting team. The tide of the war in the tri-border area (the area near the borders of Laos, Cambodia, and Vietnam – the military jargon for this area was II Corps) was only turned by the use of hundreds of B52 Arclight flights. Mr. Vann used them extensively until his death right before I was sent back to the States. These were devastating to the North Vietnamese and Vann was relentless with his use of them.

CHAPTER FORTY EIGHT:
TROOP MORALE SUFFERS

Morale is Bad and Racial Tensions are High

Back at Lane Heliport at the end of our daily missions life went on.

However, things were not all well with the morale of the U.S. Army at Lane Army Heliport. Racial tension was high. Not that I saw any racist activities, in fact I never saw any my entire 12 months in Vietnam.

But men of color were very anti-authoritarian. With Martin Luther King's assassination and the rise of the Black Power movement there was a terrible shift in attitude among some black soldiers.

So if you were an officer you would get "the look" or as some of my buddies would say, the "stink eye." This never seemed to be true among the air crew members themselves. We were pretty integrated as a group and maintained a high level of trust and respect for each other regardless of color or background. Our lives depended on it.

But the animosity got pretty bad during the last month of my tour from those other than the air crews like the cooks and other support troops. So much so that I had to sleep with my gas mask under my pillow. We were regularly gassed with CS grenades (a very potent form of tear gas) by our own troops.

Unfortunately this activity did not stop after I left the unit. About a week after my tour ended our XO was "fragged" by an unhappy soldier who waited until the XO retired to his hooch and then tossed in a grenade. The XO did not stand a chance in this senseless murder. But that was Vietnam. A lot of it just did not make sense.

Chapter Forty Nine:

Going Home!

1LT Lackey - "You're going home Crigs!"

Everybody had a calendar in Vietnam. 365 days that you counted off backwards until your tour was done. I stopped counting after 350 days. I was just mentally and emotionally whipped. I was done.

I relished the no fly days due to weather or maxing out flight time. I wrote to Diane and advised her that I should be home within the month and would call her when I got to Chicago. I still needed to do the right thing. I also chain smoked Marlboro cigarettes. I was up to three packs a day.

But the flying continued. Except something was very different.

Because of the great pilots that had mentored me I too had become an excellent pilot, as much, or even more so, than the Cavalry captain that I so admired with his flying skills early in my tour.

Now our flight movements were ever so slight. I would just "think" of a flight maneuver and the bird would react to my thought and slight movement. The helicopter became part of us like a fine instrument does with a master musician. I too was now mentoring new pilots.

One day, after about 30 resupply flights, I was counting my hash marks on the windshield and recording our flight time. I had just lit a cigarette when I saw my roommate LT Lackey in a brisk walk over to our bird.

"You're going home Crigs! You survived you sorry bastard!" he said. "You leave tomorrow and have orders for Ft Benning, GA."

He pulled his camera out and took a picture of me for posterity.

"At last," I thought. I could not wipe the smile off of my face.

Orders to Ft Benning

That night at the O Club it was bittersweet. Several of us got orders for the flight home within a couple of days of each other. Dennis Faucher got orders to Ft Hood, TX. He was assigned to A Troop 7/17 Air Cavalry. The same unit I first served with in Phan Rang. Augie Bailey would be assigned there as well. WO1 Dana Amos, WO1 Larry McKean, WO1 Don Miller and I received orders to Ft Benning, GA to fly with the 121st Aviation Company, the Flying Tigers.

That night I gifted my room to LT Lackey. I was thankful for his company and his clever wit during the months after Tom was killed. I did not care about the money anymore.

The next morning I packed my belongings in a duffle bag and headed down to the flight line for the last time. I stopped off at HQ and said farewell and thanked the commander. Then, hurrying down to the flight line I hopped in the cargo bay of a

Huey that was waiting to take me to Qui Nhon airfield. WO1 Amos was on board as well.

I don't remember who the pilots were in that Huey but they gave us one hell of a farewell ride to Qui Nhon. Low level high speed pop ups and hairpin turns and anything else to ensure that we would not forget this last Huey ride in Vietnam. And neither of us would ever forget it.

The Flight Home - The Freedom Bird

We caught a C-130 flight to Tan Son Nhut Airport in Saigon for processing out of Vietnam. I don't remember much except that we had some paperwork to fill out and then just wait until a flight was available back to the U.S.A.

Dana and I spent the next night at the O Club on base. There was no way I was going into Saigon City given the level of enemy activity in the rest of the country.

After a fitful and anxious night of sleep, finally, we found ourselves in a line of servicemen boarding a Pan American 707 for the flight back home.

Some, like Dana and myself, were in dirty jungle fatigues. Many others were in crisp khaki uniforms. These were the REMFs that typically did not face combat. But we all wanted to go home.

This flight would take us to Travis Air Force base in Northern California after a refueling stop in Yakota, Japan.

Like the trip to Vietnam, the trip home was just as packed. In fact it may have been the same plane. But the mood was much different. The men on board were anxious and it showed. Many of us were in combat operations and some had bandages to prove it.

For me, I was just a wreck. Flying around for a year with thousands of people aiming and firing weapons at you can make one very cautious and very paranoid. I was such an emotional wreck that my skin was crawling. I just wanted OUT of Vietnam.

As the Freedom Bird taxied out for takeoff the soldiers were very quiet. But once the wheels were up and the plane climbed and turned out over the South China Sea a cheer went up that lasted for five minutes. Whistling, applauding, wild laughing, and hollering as hundreds of soldiers were on their way home to what we all called "the world."

The flight seemed as long or longer than the flight we originally took to Vietnam. Except this time we were not the newbie cherries that had never seen combat. We were going back to our loved ones and family.

Most of the guys returning milled around the plane in groups talking about new assignments or perhaps their ETS (estimated termination of service from military duty) to get out. Many on the plane would be getting out of the service within weeks of their arrival back in the States.

But we all noticed the friendly Pan American stewardesses who seemed to love the cat calls and proposals they received as they passed constantly back and forth down the rows.

This plane was full, but I was alone. I did not want to think about the reception that I feared we would receive back in the States. I just could not get over the fact that our country, our people, would order us to war and into battle and then, when we return, chastise us for doing what we were asked to do. Surely this is a prescription for insanity.

For me, as the flight flew on I just reflected on the past year and all that had happened. The 7th Cavalry, all the great pilots in the 129th, the many close calls, the smell of death, my roommate Tom Shaw and meeting his family during his funeral escort. That mission of honor turned out to be much tougher that I had expected. Dying would have been easier. But Tom Shaw's advice and mentorship would have an effect on the rest of my life. My commitment to him had been fulfilled. But he had paid me much more in a sense with his moral guidance. Someday I would pay it forward by continuing to honor and comfort his family.

CHAPTER FIFTY: WEAR CIVILIAN CLOTHES

Travis Air Base

Sometime in the early evening we landed at Travis Air Force base in Northern California. Our gear was offloaded and we each received tickets or vouchers for the next trip home. And we were all anxious to get home.

Some guys were flying on military transports to their final destinations. Others like me would have to take a bus to San Francisco International Airport and take a commercial flight home.

"We recommend that you wear your civilian clothes if you have any," said a sergeant that was helping us with travel logistics. "Still lots of anti-war protesters and none of you guys need that shit after what you've been through," he said.

I agreed. I had the civilian clothes that I wore on the return trip to Vietnam from Tom's escort duty and changed out of my jungle fatigues and into those clothes. And I was glad that I did.

I'm Shocked at our National Attitude

The bus ride from Travis seemed shorter than it actually was. I would be taking a late night red eye flight back to Chicago O'Hare Airport. When I got to San Francisco Airport it was late in the evening and mercifully, there were not as many travelers as when WO1 Faucher and I had previously passed through.

But the looks of distain were still there for us. And there seemed to be no worry whatsoever about war or combat or death. Americans were just going about their business as if our soldiers and the war that we asked them to fight did not matter. It was as if WE did not matter. As if what we had done was all a waste of time, and effort, and lives.

I noticed a cardboard sign near a trash can. "Baby Killer" it said. I thought of the baby NVA that tried to kill us with that rocket propelled grenade. I could still see his face lying there in the grass. If America only knew what we were really going through instead of through the lens of a politically charged media.

I thought of the Shaw family and the great sacrifice that they had endured and would continue to endure. Tom believed that we were fighting communism to protect our own freedoms and way of life. I also believed that. But most Americans were tired of that line and no longer supported a war with endless death and destruction.

I was glad to board the flight to Chicago. I would never forget the treatment given to us returning war veterans by the people of San Francisco.

A Cab Ride Home

When the plane landed at O'Hare field it was 6am. My family did not know that I was arriving and this would be a surprise. I grabbed my duffle bag at the baggage claim area and grabbed a cab ride to my family's current home in Park Ridge, Illinois.

The cab driver was gruff and had that typical downtown city bred Chicago accent.

"Fuck you," he said flipping the middle finger to another cab driver that pulled in front of him. "Where you going bub?" he said.

I gave him the address and settled back for the ride. I had not slept since Vietnam as it just did not seem natural for me to fly and sleep at the same time. I was in a surreal and sleepless state of mind.

"Where you coming from?" he said.

"An Son," I said.

"What? Where's that?" he said.

"Vietnam," I said.

"Oh, you're not one of those crazies coming back from Vietnam are you?" he said.

"I'm crazy as hell and I would not give me any shit if I were you," I said.

He was silent the rest of the ride. So was I. He deserved it for being such a jerk.

A Day at Home and a Grateful Grandmother

By 7am I was knocking on my parents' door. One of my brothers answered as they were all getting ready for school.

"Jim's home!" he hollered, and with that many hugs and tears followed. I was extremely happy to be home. But I was also totally exhausted. I collapsed into the spare bedroom and fell into a deep sleep. I was so tired. Had it all been a dream?

Later that day and late in the afternoon I woke up. My body clock was totally out of whack having traveled from the other side of the world and through all of those time zones. My internal clock was still on Vietnam time.

My grandmother, now living with my parents, was waiting to talk to me when I awoke.

"Jimmy I prayed for you every day," she said.

"And I said the Lord's Prayer on every takeoff and every landing Grandma. And I kept that lucky rosary with me on every flight," I said.

She was so grateful that I was alive. The two of us just hugged and cried tears of happiness. I had survived.

A Trip to Frank and Ginny Shaw

I stayed at my parents' house for two days. Mostly I caught up on my sleep and just enjoyed eating home cooked meals with my family.

I had two weeks leave before I had to be at Ft Benning and there was much to do. But before I did anything to solve my personal issues I needed to see Tom's parents, Frank and Ginny Shaw. They too promised to pray for my safety and asked me to let them know when I got back from Vietnam. I would do one better. I would visit them.

I called the Shaw home and when Ginny answered I asked if I could visit that day. She was delighted and said that Frank and she would love to see me.

I drove up to Fond du Lac with the mission to take them out to dinner. Tom's parents were extremely gracious to me and

I was so honored to be with these wonderful people that had sacrificed so much. But they would have nothing to do with me paying for dinner.

They took me to a wonderful country club restaurant overlooking Fond du Lac. We talked for three or four hours. When it was time to leave I felt like I was leaving a family I had known all my life. Our hearts were broken and we clearly understood each other's pain.

I am forever grateful for the kindness of Frank and Ginny Shaw. I would visit Frank and Ginny one more time when I ETS (Expiration of Term of Service) two years later to start life as a civilian again. I would not see any Shaw family member again for 37 years.

Chapter Fifty One:

Do the Right Thing

A Trip to St. Louis to FINALLY do the Right Thing

From Fond du Lac, WI I drove back to spend a late night with my brother Mike and brother John.

Mike looked like a different person with hair longer and he was now an excellent guitar player. And John had grown up since I left. It was good to hang with them as I forgot about the war that night.

Mike of course knew where I was coming from concerning Vietnam.

"Nobody cares Jim," he said. "It's a sad state that we are in."

Though he was against the war, he would have nothing to do with harassing the returning troops.

The next morning with Diane's address in hand I said farewell to my family and hopped in my car for the five hour drive to St. Louis. I was still amazed at the level of ease that everyone was in. I saw no one carry weapons. No one looked over their shoulder. No one was at war. No one except me.

Even driving I could not get over the feeling of being a target. I got out of combat just five days ago. I was sure it showed.

She Accepts - Seven Days of Macaroni and Cheese

Diane Pastors was kicked out of her home in April by her feuding and drunken mother. The parents were in a colossal divorce. Diane and Lisa unintentionally just added fuel to the fire and they were asked to leave.

I would never understand this or try to understand a mother that could turn her own daughter away. But Diane was resourceful and was able to acquire an apartment near University of Missouri, St. Louis Campus. It was a cute one bedroom apartment near a babysitter that she had found when she got a job at AT&T. And that's where I found them when I finally got to St. Louis.

I knocked on the door not quite knowing want to expect. But Diane opened the door and hugged me like I have never been hugged before. She still loved me. And I loved her. Lisa was a bonus and such a lovely baby. I fell in love with them both. Tom was right; this was not a ball and chain, but a child that would make a difference in the future. I proposed to them both. Diane accepted.

I was able to stay with Diane and Lisa for eight or nine days. We ate macaroni and cheese or pizza at every meal. Diane had figured some things out but had not figured out how to cook yet. But they both loved to eat macaroni and cheese. It was easy for her to make. And it was easy for me to stay there.

I was in bliss and for a while, I forgot about the Army and Vietnam.

But I was still not used to all the conveniences. A phone on the wall to call anyone. Hot showers. A washer AND a dryer that did not need a hooch maid. Liquor stores with cold beer. White Castles, McDonald's, Perkins, Pizza Hut and so many others.

But I still was very aware of my surroundings and always looking over my shoulder. I was tense and a little paranoid everywhere I went. I didn't sleep well at all and even Diane noticed. Several nights I woke up in a cold sweat, sweating so profusely the bed was soaked. I was not the same man I was when I left. I had survived without a scratch, but inside I was now a different person.

Chapter Fifty Two:

The 121st Aviation Company – Flying Tigers

Fort Benning, GA

Diane and I decided that I should get settled into my new assignment and that we would pick a date to get married six or seven months from then. It was late September or early October of 1972.

I made the ten hour drive to Columbus, GA and Fort Benning on the last day of my leave and reported for duty at the 121st Aviation Company the next day.

The 121st Tigers had originally been in Vietnam in the III Corps or the Delta region to the south of where I was stationed. In Vietnam they were called the Soc Trang Tigers. But they had stood down earlier than the 7/17th Cav and found a home at the Army Ranger and Jump School in Fort Benning. I settled in to a room at the BOQ (bachelor officer quarters).

The next day I met the company commander and my platoon leader Captain Ron Stokes. They were happy to have another experienced Vietnam pilot and commented on how many 129th pilots were being transferred to the unit. There were also other pilots that were in my flight class that flew in Vietnam but not with the 129th that were there as well. WO1 Herb Koenig was our class valedictorian who had been assigned to the 60th Assault Helicopter Company in II Corps just south of my AO.

Like me with the 7/17th Cav he flew very little during the first four months in Vietnam. The 60th also was tasked with training ARVN pilots. With all the lousy jobs already assigned at the 60th (like Tech Supply Officer), Herb was forced to be the unit bartender. That is until three months later when the company realized that all the Aircraft Commanders were finishing their Vietnam Tour of duty. Then, like me, the 60th flew the hell out of him the rest of his tour. I'm sure that bartending was tough duty though as drunken "short timer" pilots could be pretty cruel to the newbie cherry pilots whether they bartended or not.

Training with the Airborne Rangers

I settled in to life with the 121st pretty well. Most of the Vietnam pilots were given check rides from the unit IP. Since our flying skills were high comparable to the other pilots we were made unit aircraft commanders, so I would continue flying from the left seat.

Flying Hueys back in the United States was very different from flying in Vietnam. Here we had all the rules and FAA regulations. All of us had to study up on these to remain current with our airport protocols and flight rule knowledge.

Flying was not as rigorous either. Typically we would fly 25 to 30 hours per month vs six to ten hours (or more) per day in Vietnam. The week usually consisted of morning briefings followed by a card game followed by an early release of any pilot not flying missions that day, which was most of us.

With the exception of supporting the Rangers it was pretty boring compared to the life and death excitement that we had lived just a month prior.

The Army Rangers were an elite fighting group and trained in Ft Benning as well as a small ranger base in the North Georgia mountains near Dahlonega, GA. I loved flying in the mountains and hovering over peaks and near cliffs where the Rangers would repel out of our ships. We also supported many training missions in and around the base at Ft Benning.

An Officer's Club Card that is Also a VISA Card

The O Club at Benning was nice. But it had way too much pomp and circumstance for my blood after spending so much time at the Lane O Club. I spent very little time at the Benning O Club other than required meetings of our unit officer corps.

But the big advantage of being an officer with an O Club access was that the club card was actually a VISA Card with a six thousand dollar limit. This was the first time in my life that I had a credit card in my pocket.

Living with Dana Amos

One of my flight school and 129th cohorts also shared a room at the BOQ. WO1 Dana Amos needed a roommate for a townhouse that he wanted to move into. I volunteered.

Dana was as smart as a whip but he did not have a lot of flight time from the 129th in Vietnam and I never really knew why as his only extra duty was unknown to me. Since we both had massive stereo systems purchased through the PACEX catalog we had some pretty good music to listen to.

And that is ALL that Dana did. He would get home from our brief day at the 121st, turn on the music and waste the day away. When Friday came he was gone at noon to go back to his family home about an hour away. Then he would return in time for the 8am Monday briefing. He was basically an absent roommate and one I would not get close with. I became friends with Johnny Walker Red scotch.

CHAPTER FIFTY THREE: AN UNEXPECTED TRIP TO ST. LOUIS

Paranoid and a Pistol from Walmart

Having the convenience of a phone in our townhouse I talked to Diane at least every other day until about mid-October. Then without reason her phone was constantly busy. As if the phone was off hook on purpose.

There were no voice mail capabilities in 1972 so if you did not answer your phone you got no message. It was frustrating. But I would still end up talking to her periodically.

I also tried to get in touch with Linda Van Hurst. But the phone was disconnected when I called. So I decided to write Linda and tell her the truth, apologize, and offer help. I spent the better part of a weekend drinking scotch and writing and re-writing that letter. I sent it to the address that I met her at in May.

In spite of not being in a war zone I still had this nagging feeling of vulnerability. Always looking over my shoulder and being super aware of my circumstances. And I had no protection. After wearing a .38 caliber pistol and carrying a CAR 15 with 200 rounds of ammo with me for the better part of a year I missed not being able to return fire if necessary. So one day at the Walmart store I plopped down fifty bucks for an Iver Johnson .25 caliber pistol. It wasn't much, just a little Saturday night special. But it made me feel a little safer. I would sleep with that gun under my pillow or carry it in my pocket for many years.

Highly Skilled Pilots

It amazed me how good we Vietnam pilots had become at "seat of the pants" flying. If I was flying with another Vietnam pilot it did not show. But many of our missions included captains and 1LTs that were not members of the 121st but rather in desk jobs.

These men had to maintain their flight proficiency and were required to fly at least four hours per month. It was our job to keep these pilots current and comfortable flying, which most of them were not. Typically they could not hover worth a damn. But frankly, it wasn't their fault. It's damned hard to maintain your comfort level at flying and hovering a helicopter with such minimal flight time. But without bullets flying at us we could afford to be patient and let these flyers gain at least some of their skills back.

An Unexpected Leave at Thanksgiving and More Busy Signals

Since I had no leave time left I was assigned to work as standby pilot for the weekend of Thanksgiving.

But unexpectedly our flight platoon leader, Captain Stokes, gave us the time off and said, "Look, you guys spent the last Thanksgiving in Vietnam. I'm covering for you this weekend. Go home and see your family."

I was extremely grateful. It was Wednesday morning and I quickly hopped in my Corvette and drove to my apartment to grab a coat and small carry on duffle bag with a change of clothes. I grabbed my pistol and put it in my coat pocket. Then I sped off to Columbus Airport and got on the military standby waiting list for flights to connect to St. Louis.

From the airport I tried calling Diane. I made three, four, maybe even five attempts to call her on a pay phone. Each time was met with a busy signal. I did not care though; I was going to see her anyway. I believed that she would be happy to see me, even if I surprised her. In retrospect, I should have seen the writing on the wall.

Standby Flight to St. Louis, Snowstorm and an Act of Kindness

I had to wait two flights before a standby seat opened up to Atlanta to transfer to a St. Louis flight. I had missed the first connection out of Atlanta but made the second connection as they were closing the doors of the aircraft after last boarding call. It was 8pm Eastern time and a three hour flight to St. Louis. With luck I would be there at 10pm local time. But luck would not be with us. On this Wednesday evening in 1972 a snowstorm would hit St. Louis. The plane was delayed by almost two hours.

Fortunately I sat next to an older gentleman who was NOT an anti-war type. He pegged me as a military guy because of my short hair and started to ask questions about what I did in the service. When the subject came to Vietnam he plied me with questions on the war. I had been out of combat for less than two months. We talked for the better part of two hours. The fellow was quite courteous and even offered to give me a ride to Diane's apartment just a few miles from the Lambert International Airport. I gladly accepted his act of kindness.

The ride to Diane's apartment was rough. The weather was terrible with large heavy snowflakes falling. The snowplows had not caught up with the side roads yet and this kind man had some difficulty maneuvering his rear wheel drive sedan through eight inches of snow on the road. But after much wheel spinning and swerving we finally made it. I thanked him and had to give him a push to get him going out of the parking lot. It was a few minutes before midnight.

A Knock on the Door with No Reply

It was freezing outside and I was wet with the large snowflakes falling on me. I saw Diane's car in the parking lot and was relieved to know that at least she should be home. But I did not see any lights on in the apartment.

I opened the door to the apartment vestibule and got out of the storm. It felt good to be warm in that hallway. I shook the snow off of my coat and clothes and gained a little composure from the cold.

"Knock, knock, knock."

There was no doorbell so I knocked on the door with my knuckles.

I waited about thirty seconds and knocked again, "Knock, knock, knock."

Still no answer.

One of the neighbors stuck his head out of his door wondering who would be knocking on apartment doors at midnight in this storm.

"Sorry, Diane's not expecting me. It's a surprise. She's probably asleep," I said.

He nodded and closed the door to his apartment. I waited thirty more seconds.

"Knock, knock, knock."

This time I heard movement in the apartment and a door close.

"Who is it?" asked Diane.

"It's me honey. It's Jim. I've been calling you all day. I got an unexpected holiday leave and caught a flight. Your phone was busy all day," I said.

"Go away," she said

"What? What do you mean go away?" I said.

The chain lock slid off to hang on the wall and the door slowly opened.

"You can't come in. What are you doing here anyway?" she said.

"Look I'm sorry, I tried to call you but your phone was busy all day. Finally I just decided to surprise you and Lisa," I said.

She opened the door and let me come in. I could see the phone dangling off the hook of its wall mount.

"Well there's the problem. Your phone is off the hook. Can I use your bathroom? I haven't gone since Atlanta," I said.

Then I noticed the bathroom door closed with the light on and noticed a shadow move on the crack at the bottom of the door.

"NO!" she said, almost screaming.

"Wait a minute Diane," I said, "who is in your bathroom?"

"Just get out, please get out," she said.

"Oh no, is there a guy in your bathroom?!" I said.

"Just leave," she said and held the door open.

I looked over at the hanging phone. Then I turned and looked at the bathroom door.

The Ultimate Payback as Whoever He is Hides in the Bathroom

As I walked out the front door Diane, without a word, shut and locked the door behind me. I was never so dejected or rejected in my life. I was numb as I walked out the opposite door of the vestibule that I had entered. This one had steps leading down to the street level sidewalk.

I sat down on the top step in eight inches of wet snow and cried. The snowflakes were still coming down large and wet. You could not see across the street.

"The ultimate payback," I thought. "This I brought on myself with my lack of courage and action." I was in a place of deep and dark despair. It was then that I reached into my coat pocket and pulled out my pistol. I cocked the hammer and put it up to my temple.

It's Over

I sat there shaking, the snow falling, the cocked pistol held fast to my head. And all I could think of was that I had survived the war but I would not survive my own stupidity.

Words ran through my mind. I drifted off mentally into a place that I had never been before. But one sentence appeared over and over like a neon sign in my brain.

"You cannot do this to yourself. THIS is not the right thing."

Over and over this would repeat in my mind until finally, covered in wet snow, I lowered the pistol. Then I looked at my watch. It was 12:45am. I must have been sitting on that step in the snow for thirty minutes. Perhaps it was the cold or maybe just that little voice in my head that caused me to act. But now I needed to get out of there. With no phone and no car and in a snowstorm I was stranded.

I Get My Composure and Call a Friend

With no choice but to sleep in the vestibule or call a friend I walked back in and knocked on Diane's front door.

"I'm sorry to bother you Diane but I don't have a choice. There is a snowstorm and I need to use your phone to call a friend and see if I can get a ride. Please let me use your phone," I said.

"Just a minute," said Diane.

I heard a little commotion and then the bathroom door shut. Then the front door opened.

"You can use the phone over there," she said.

I looked at the phone on the wall and it had been returned to its receiver. I picked it up and dialed the only friend that I had a phone number for.

I had not spoken to Roger Schuster since I left for Vietnam. Now I would be calling him at one in the morning.

"Hello?"

"Roger, it's Jim Crigler and I need your help," I said.

I explained my situation and to my great relief he said, "Gimme the address, I'll be right there."

I thanked Diane, took another look at the bathroom door, and left. I never knew the name of the guy behind that door. But 20 years from that night I would meet him face to face.

Roger "The Dodger" Schuster

I waited in the heated apartment vestibule and in about 15 minutes Roger drove up. It was easy to see him as there were zero cars driving in this storm and at this hour so early in the morning.

I felt empty and numb as I walked out to his car in the parking lot. I had met Roger several years prior when I was in high school. He was a high school dropout and a pretty wild character. On Saturday nights he liked to drive around the north side of St. Louis with a baseball bat and knock car side mirrors off as he drove past. Back then he was a real juvenile delinquent. Everybody called him "Roger The Dodger" because he never got in trouble for his crazy antics.

But a two year stint in the Army as a truck driver in Germany set him on the right track in life.

"Crigler!" he said. "What the hell have you been doing? I haven't heard from you in over a year."

I thanked him for picking me up at this late hour. He would take me to his house just a few miles away in Ferguson, MO. As we drove I told him that I had just gotten back from Vietnam a few months prior.

"I fucked up bad Roger," I said. "Because of my inaction and lack of courage to do the right thing I lost not only a fiancée tonight but a daughter as well."

As we drove through the snow I told him the story. When we got to his home his wife was waiting. She had put a pillow and some blankets on the couch for me to bed down. But there was no way that I could sleep. For the rest of the night I stayed up talking with Roger about Vietnam and my crazy predicament.

I must have looked terrible. Still damp from sitting on the snowy steps and broken hearted I was just a mess. Many times that night the emotions welled up in me such that I could not speak. I had been back from combat fewer than three months. As we talked it got light out in the early morning and the snow stopped. It was Thanksgiving Day 1972.

Standby Flight Back to Fort Benning

Roger's wife insisted that I stay with them for the Thanksgiving holiday. But I declined. In my numb and depressed state I felt nothing to be thankful for. Roger offered to take me to the airport that morning and I gladly accepted.

At the airport we said our farewells and I promised to look him up when I got out of the service. It was fewer than eight hours since I landed the previous evening and I was now standing in line to get a flight back to Columbus, GA airport.

As it was Thanksgiving the passenger traffic was much lighter than the previous day. I was able to get a military standby on the first flight out to Atlanta. I arrived back at Columbus airport just before dark.

I had not eaten since the previous day. And I was not hungry now. I opened the door to my Corvette and slid into the seat. My hands were shaking. My mind was numb.

When I got back to my townhome it was empty. My roommate Dana had left the previous Tuesday to go home to his parents' house and visit friends. I was alone. I put on some music and opened a new bottle of Johnny Walker Red scotch. The Moody Blues sang *Nights in White Satin.* I drank. I thought of my roommate Tom Shaw. How different he was than Dana Amos.

Tom was right. Each time we run into a wall in life the road we travel has a fork in it. Which fork we choose will have an enormous impact on our lives. But that night, on an empty stomach and emotionally drained, I just drank. It was as if I was having my own Irish wake for a love that died. That night a little of me died as well.

CHAPTER FIFTY FOUR:
SELF-MEDICATION

I Self-Medicate

The next day, like the Irish wakes at the 129th in Vietnam, I woke up on the floor. It was Friday, the day after Thanksgiving, and there was much movement in Columbus, Georgia and at Fort Benning. The Christmas shopping season was now in full swing.

As I woke up I took four aspirin to relieve the pounding in my head. I remembered the evening prior to Thanksgiving though and my heart ached. My stomach was nonexistent and I was still not hungry.

I took a quick shower and got dressed. It was 11am. Then I hopped in my car and drove to the Fort Benning Post Exchange or PX. I was still smoking through an average of three and sometimes four packs of Marlboro cigarettes a day and I was almost out. And I needed more scotch.

I bought three cartons of cigarettes and three quart bottles of Johnny Walker with my O Club credit card. After paying for the flights to and from St. Louis I was broke. But that awful weekend

I just smoked and drank. I did not eat until Sunday after I had gone without food for almost four days. Finally, on Sunday, broke and out of scotch, I was forced to sober up. I tried to call Diane but the phone was once again off the hook and I got nothing but busy signals.

A Returned Letter

On Monday I was at the morning pilots briefing at the 121st operations hangar wondering where Dana Amos was. It turned out that he had taken an extra day of leave and did not get back to Benning until late afternoon.

Thankfully I was assigned to Ranger training missions all day and would get quite a bit of flight time. The last thing I needed was to be alone in my townhouse. The comradery of the crew and the constant action of Ranger troops going through exercises was a pleasant relief from the boredom and heartache I felt during the weekend. It was also good to be at the controls of the Huey and feel the air as we flew our missions.

I was flying with WO1 Mike Butler who was right out of flight school.

When we finally shut down for the day it was getting dusk. When I got back to my townhouse Dana was already there. He was blaring some new music he picked up.

"Hey roomie, I got a letter for you. It was in the mail box when I got here this afternoon," he said as he handed me the letter.

It was the letter that I had sent to Linda 10 days prior. It was unopened and had a Post Office inked stamp on it: "No such person at this address."

"What the hell," I thought, "I couldn't even get that right."

Not remembering everything that I had written I opened the letter and re-read my words. The letter was terribly composed and the words awkward. I was embarrassed and thanked God that Linda had not seen this letter. Scotch does NOT make a good writing partner.

But I vowed to make it right. In spite of my rejection by Diane I still owed it to Linda to be truthful. But for now I needed to heal. I poured three fingers of scotch in a glass and added ice.

I Need Some Help But Don't Get It

My drinking was now pretty much out of control. It was as bad as or maybe even worse than any of the times in Vietnam. Most days we did not fly. Compared to the massive amount of flight time and excitement of constantly being on the go with resupply or combat missions in Vietnam this was pretty boring.

Several times I thought of ending my life. One Saturday night I got particularly drunk. As usual, Dana was gone to his parents' home for the weekend. I had been flying for six hours that day taking the parachute jump team up to 10 or 12,000 feet. Up and down all day long. It was our most boring mission.

But I turned it into a training mission for my co-pilot Mike Butler and taught him combat corkscrew landings just like Augie Bailey had taught me. And the parachute team noticed because we actually beat them to the ground. But that night I was not celebrating corkscrew landings, I was lamenting on my mistakes in life.

I grabbed a piece of paper and wrote a suicide note to my mother. Then in a drunken stupor I put a stamp on the addressed envelope, stumbled out to the mailbox, flipped the red flag up for mail pickup and went back into the house to drink. I woke up the next day with a cocked pistol next to my pillow and an empty scotch bottle on the floor. I was a mess. And I had no recollection of writing or mailing a suicide note.

Six days later I was getting ready to leave my home for the morning pilots' briefing when my mom and my brother John showed up at my front door. They did not call on the phone first, they just showed up.

My mom had gotten my drunken suicide note and grabbed my 16 year old brother John to help her drive all night from Chicago to Fort Benning, GA. My mother never mentioned the note that I had sent her. In fact, she never mentioned anything about it for 40 years. (I only found the note because she had saved it with all my Vietnam correspondence). She just said she wanted to make sure that I was OK and give me some home cooking. They stayed a week.

A Red Rose Every Day

The day after they left I went to my morning flight briefing. This was a no flying day so I had the afternoon off. I made the decision that I would not give up on Diane. I may have fucked up royally by waiting so long but I owed it to myself and Lisa and Diane to try to make it right. So I called a florist in Ferguson, Missouri and scheduled a single red rose to be delivered every day with a card that simply said, "I apologize for how this has turned out, I love you, Jim."

The florist would charge my VISA card and agreed to deliver to Diane's apartment every day for at least two months. In the mean time I would write to Diane and see if I could fix what I had broken.

For a month I would write Diane two or three times a week. If I could not call her at least I would write and try a one way communication. I never got a reply.

Five weeks after I started sending the roses I got a call one evening from the florist. It was the lady that I had first given my order to.

She said, "Jim, I'm sorry to call you as I would really like to keep your business but the money you are paying me is being wasted. I've seen the roses simply thrown in the dumpster unopened outside of Diane's apartment for weeks and today there was a note taped on the door that asked me not to deliver any additional flowers. I'm sorry Jim but I can't in good faith take your money."

I thanked her for calling. I had to face the facts. I had waited too long. In the scheme of things people come into and out of your life, whether it's a friend, mentor, or a lover. A new love had come into her life. Clearly this was the case or she would have at least replied to me. As dejected as I was I had to face this truth.

Chapter Fifty Five:
A New Mentor

A New Roommate

I'm not sure whether I was the problem or Dana. It was probably both of us. But we were not getting along well as roommates. Dana was a little pissed that my mom and brother had stayed a week. But for me it was the break from alcohol that I needed. And one of the things I needed most was a new roommate.

At the morning briefings the pilots usually milled around discussing areas of operations or playing cards in the pilots lounge. This morning I was playing cards with a group of warrants including WO1 Herb Koenig.

"I'm getting kind of tired of the officers BOQ," he said. "Any of you guys looking for a roommate?"

"Sure," I said, "let's talk later about what you are looking to do."

So later that morning Herb and I discussed a possible roommate situation over coffee. Herb was from the south side of Chicago and of modest means. He was drafted at the age of 23 and was one of the oldest guys in our flight class. He was also the smartest guy in our flight class, graduating number one out of 98 students. Like me he had tested into the Warrant Officer Flight program. He was a bourbon drinker.

As Dana and I were on a month to month lease I gave him notice and Herb and I moved into a house on the east side of Columbus, GA.

Herb was a great roommate, and like Tom Shaw, a good mentor. His plan was to get out of the Army as soon as possible and go back to college and get his degree. He was an excellent influence on me and I made plans to do the same. The GI Bill would be an excellent and well-earned benefit for us both.

Life Goes on One Day at a Time

My memory is sketchy but sometime during the beginning of 1973 I told Linda the truth. It was awkward but she deserved to know the whole story. From that point on I saw neither Linda or Diane. Both would disappear from my life.

Though I still drank too much, Herb and the U.S. Army became a stabilizing factor in my life. And though I was still heartbroken and impacted by my time in Vietnam, life would go on one day at a time.

Brother Mike Dies

By June of 1973 I was getting used to having a direction back in my life. I had slowed my drinking down to a normalcy, or at least normal for a warrant officer in 1973. Herb and I had become good friends.

I even started to date again. Life was starting to bloom again.

On June 13th I was visiting a pilot friend, WO1 Bud Downing, who wanted to introduce me to his sister-in-law. While at Bud's house I got a phone call from Herb. It was probably the toughest call he ever had to make.

"Jim," he said, "I'm sorry to tell you this but your brother Mike has been killed in an automobile accident."

I stood there in shock. Then I dropped the phone on the floor and just cried. The brother that I had lived in the same room with all my life until we both left for the service was dead. The victim of a Chicago driver. I was devastated. He had survived the war, even made his stance against the war, but he did not survive the traffic of Chicago.

After the funeral in Park Ridge, IL I returned to Fort Benning. Thank God for Herb Koenig as he was a big reason that I did not fall off the emotional cliff again. Losing my brother made me sit up straighter in life.

I realized that death was not just in Vietnam. Life was precious and could be gone in an instant. No matter where you are.

In the summer of 1973 both Herb and I were promoted to CW2. In late 1973 CW2 Herb Koenig applied for and got an early ETS. He moved back to the Chicago south side and eventually got an engineering degree from University of Illinois at Chicago Circle Campus.

CHAPTER FIFTY SIX:

THE IMPACT OF WAR

The Power of War and Combat on One's Psyche

After Herb moved back to Chicago I got a one bedroom apartment down by the Chattahoochee River near Downtown Columbus, GA. I was now dating Bud Downing's sister-in-law Susan and was actively flying Ranger missions to Dahlonega, GA.

I also spent several months as a test pilot TDY (temporary duty status in which the Army pays you an extra stipend to live in a remote area from your base) at an Army depot near Atlanta.

Living alone gave me plenty of time to think. I was definitely impacted by Vietnam and the mood of the United States public compounded these effects. I came to realize that you cannot send a man or woman into combat and ever expect them to be the same person they were prior. War is a change agent. It had changed me drastically.

And it seemed to impact everyone different. Herb was not really affected. Neither, it seemed at the time, was Dana Amos. But I now had a different sense of the world around me and it would influence my life from that moment on.

The Impact of a Lost Pilot's Words and the Direction That it Gave Me

I also realized the great impact that my roommate Tom Shaw had on my life thus far. Until Tom's mentorship I had been a real "feather in the wind" and had not had much direction in my life. Wherever the winds of life blew me, I went.

But through Tom's impact I came to realize that having a plan or direction in life was very important. And now I could anticipate my direction knowing that life will always go down a path that leads to a fork in the road. There are choices that we will have to make and some of those choices will be hard. It takes courage to choose a fork in the path, especially if it's that hard path, but the right path.

I also remembered the entire moral compass that he had given to me. Courage. Focus on what is right in life not what is wrong. Be truthful. Trust in your God.

I came to understand that having courage meant many things. Having the courage to fly into a hail of bullets was one thing. But having the courage to forgive was yet another. I would always keep Tom's compass with me.

Later in life it would give me the courage to forgive Diane. Even the man in the bathroom that snowy night. I forgave him too. But most of all, and the toughest person to forgive, was myself. I had made some horrible mistakes that had impacted the lives of wonderful people.

A Life of Learning and Mistakes

I got out of the Army in August of 1974. In January 1975 I started my second college attempt at the University of Missouri at St.

Louis. This time I applied myself and dove into my studies. I was determined to learn.

With the exception of a brief time joining the Vietnam Veterans against the War, I rarely spoke of my time in Vietnam. The war in Vietnam, at least for the United States troops, ended in the spring of 1973. But the final invasion by the North and the fall of Saigon did not happen until mid-1975.

After President Nixon's impeachment the U.S. Congress refused to keep its promise to Vietnam and stopped funding the war effort. With no supplies or parts it was only a matter of time before Ho Chi Minh would invade. The war ended nevertheless.

For me, I just wanted to move forward. I buried the war, or at least most of it, in the dark recesses of my mind. I would now focus on what was right, not what was wrong with the world.

I also made many attempts to find Diane as well as Linda. I owed those children my knowledge and much more as they would be difference makers in the future. But to no avail. With the exception of a brief phone discussion with Linda, and a failure on my part, I would not see either of these children for many years.

But as it always does, life would go on. In November 1977 I married Susan Sirry, Bud Downing's sister-in-law. We started a life together that would last for twelve years and blossomed two wonderful children.

After 36 months of college at the University of Missouri I would graduate with a Bachelor of Science in Business Management. Because of my training in flight school and my intense determination to focus on studies I graduated magna cum laude. I would then use the rest of my GI Bill to make it most of the way through my MBA. I would not finish.

I would make much headway in my life in the years to come. I would also make many mistakes. But that is how life works. It's not all positive and moving forward. Humans learn by making mistakes and figuring how to correct them. The more mistakes, the more you learn. I would learn a lot.

I also often thought about our great country and the political, military, and civics mistakes that we had made.

What had we learned as a nation from our involvement in Vietnam? It seemed to me that we had learned little, especially in our treatment of those that we asked, or forced, to fight the war. The perception of the Vietnam veteran, at least as perpetuated by the press, changed very little. Even though most Vietnam vets were just like me. We worked hard, climbed the corporate ladders, and did fairly well. Most Vietnam veterans that I knew were much better off than their counterparts.

But we were still made out to be somewhat crazy. It's true. War will change you. You will never be the same. THAT is what happens when you send a human into combat and they see the ugliness of war. Call it shell shock, call it Post Traumatic Stress, or call it whatever you like. The fact is that those memories NEVER go away. They are now part of you. Most Vietnam veterans get that.

But the lack of honor of their sacrifice, especially of the Gold Star Families' sacrifices was the toughest for most of us to take. For me, it took a couple of years, but I finally got it. The Vietnam War was whatever it was. We can't change the past. But we can improve on our future. And we can still honor those that gave the most. By honoring those people that impacted our lives, like the soldiers on the Vietnam Veterans Memorial Wall or those that are left behind, like the Gold Star Families, we ourselves will be living a life of honor. And that discovery, at least for me, was a game changer. 

Throughout the past several years I have taken it upon myself to speak up and talk about the Vietnam War. I have emerged from my forty years silence. I have spoken at many veteran and memorial events and at colleges and high schools. 

One of the things I have discovered is that our Gold Star Families have mostly been forgotten, especially our Vietnam Gold Star Families. Most of these families, after death notification and burial of their loved ones, just did not talk about it anymore. They, like me and many other Vietnam veterans, had buried it due to the controversial nature of that war.

But this is just not right. As a free country we owe it to those families that have sacrificed so much for our freedoms to give them a high level of honor and respect. As for me I now know my next path in life. I am on a mission to start a national movement to make that happen; to let our Gold Star Families know that they are not forgotten and that their great sacrifice is appreciated.

It can be as simple as a short letter, a card, an email, or even a brief phone call to thank them for their great sacrifice. It does not have to be much. But it does have to be something. We owe this to EVERY Gold Star Family in our country. This should be every American's mission. I know it will be mine.

EPILOGUE

After I got out of the Army and over the next 15 or so years I concentrated on making a life for myself, my wife Susan, and my son and daughter.

Money was tight and the work hours were long. In 1981 I entered the world of telecommunications just as it was deregulating in the United States and began a journey to climb the corporate ladder in that industry. As I worked and traveled I continued to look for Linda and Diane and my two daughters. But in the days prior to the internet it was pretty easy to disappear if one wanted to.

In 1983 I moved to Chicago. This was a city that, after my brother Mike was killed, I swore I would never return to. But Chicago turned out to be the right fork in the road of life for me to take. I excelled at my work and I came to love the city and the hard working people that lived in it.

In 1986 a friend told me about a welcome home parade for Vietnam Veterans that Chicago Mayor Harold Washington was going to put on for those veterans. Though I had buried Vietnam long ago I still had part of me that did not feel right about the war. Like a nagging ache in my soul. I decided to march in that parade.

On June 13th, 1986, the same day my brother Mike died 13 years prior, I put my Vietnam flight suit on and drove downtown to march in that parade. I was 36 years old.

When I arrived at the parade, I found only one other pilot out of the thousands of men that were marching. His name was Al Fischer and he flew with the 101st Aviation, call sign "Kingsmen" at Camp Eagle in I Corps along the DMZ in Vietnam. He was one of the pilots that survived LAM SON 719. He also wore his Vietnam flight suit.

Al and I marched in the parade side by side and every Chicago bar we passed brought us out a beer. By the time the parade ended we were pretty inebriated. But we continued to drink.

At the end of the parade the city of Chicago had set up beer and food booths and also had one of the new replicas of the Vietnam Wall that was just recently dedicated in Washington DC. As both of us looked on at the Moving Wall we fell in each other's drunken arms and cried like babies for maybe 20 minutes. Each of us remembering our friends and comrades that were either killed or affected by that war. For both of us it would be the beginning of a healing process.

In 1989 my 80 hour work weeks finally took a toll on my marriage and Susan left me for the relatively stress free lifestyle of country living. We were divorced in January 1989. I had become a very focused workaholic.

But I had also earned and saved my money. I now had enough spare cash to hire a private investigator to help me find Linda and Diane. I was determined to make things right and be a father to my daughters if they wanted me. Ten thousand dollars later I still had not found Linda but the investigator did find Diane's mother. She was living in St. Charles, Missouri.

She pleaded with the private investigator to tell me not to get in touch with Diane's family. They had never told my daughter Lisa about me and, according to Mrs. Pastors, my contact with the family would only harm Lisa. I had reached another fork in my path of life. I decided that I would not contact this family. The last thing I wanted to do was bring discord into my daughter's life.

I wrote Mrs. Pastors a long letter telling her of my life and assuring her that I would not disturb her daughter's family. Then I added that if they ever did want to reach me they could. I left all of my contact information for her to have.

Also in 1989 I visited my grandparents in St. Louis, Missouri. These were my Dad's parents. As young children we had spent very little time with this side of my family. But perhaps with age, we grew closer. My grandfather had the same name as my dad and me. I am James lll.

I wanted to videotape them and get their perspective on life before they passed. After the videotaping I talked to them about my mission to find my daughters. They were one of those couples that had been in the phone book for years and I wanted them to stay in that print until I found my daughter Carrie. If Linda ever was looking to find me she only needed look in the phone book and would find my grandparents. It was just in case. While I was talking to them the phone rang and my grandmother went in the other room to answer it. A few minutes later she returned with an ashen look on her face.

"Jimmy, I think your daughter is on the phone!" she said. "She wants to talk to me and I want you to listen on the other phone."

So I grabbed another extension and unscrewed the mouthpiece to mute the phone and listened in on the call. This was a strange coincidence indeed. But as I listened to the young girl tell her story something was just not right. Her mom was named Aurora. And her name was Camille. And she was born in 1959. Nothing was adding up but she insisted that her father was Jim Crigler.

My grandmother graciously took her contact phone number and assured her that she would pass it on.

I hung the phone up and walked into the room that my grandmother was in. Both of us looked at each other.

"It's my/your dad's daughter!" we both said in unison.

In what would go down in my life as one of the strangest coincidences, I now finally understood why my parents would not give me advice on my own similar issue.

In the coming weeks I would contact Camille and even visit her in San Antonio, TX. Several weeks after I met Camille I flew her to Chicago and introduced her to her brothers and sisters.

During that same meeting but a few hours later I also invited my Mom and my Dad to attend. I told them nothing of Camille.

When they arrived I introduced my dad to his daughter. He had a look of shock on his face. But my mother, God bless her, walked over to Camille, put her arms around her and said, "Welcome to the family."

Camille became, and still is, my loving sister.

About a month after my visit with my dad's parents they received an invitation to a high school graduation ceremony at Parkway High School. It was an invitation to my daughter Carrie's high school graduation.

It had no return address on it. It was sent as a joke. But they had indeed looked up the address in the St. Louis phone directory. This lead helped me to find my daughter Carrie. I even attended her high school graduation ceremony.

Linda Van Hurst had never married. When I met her again after all those years I realized that this was truly a special woman indeed. The effects of combat and the heartache of being jilted by another love so long ago had clouded my eyes to this wonderful person. We will remain friends forever.

The high school graduation invitation helped me start a loving relationship with my daughter Carrie. She needed a father. For the rest of my life I will be there for her.

Several years later I received a letter from Springfield, Missouri. It was from my daughter Lisa.

Her grandmother, after surviving breast cancer and finally sobering up, had decided to tell Lisa about me and had given her the letter that I wrote to her when the investigator found her. How ironic it was to me that the person who had treated me so miserably and blocked me at every path from Diane was now the one that chose to tell Diane's daughter Lisa that the man in the bathroom was not her father.

Lisa was in her last year of college at University of Missouri and wanted to meet me. Over the upcoming months I would meet with Lisa and also her grandmother. Mrs. Pastors was a changed woman. I was honored that she noted all the times that she had blocked me from her daughter and wished she hadn't. Her tearful apology was accepted by a tearful hug of forgiveness. But in reality I had forgiven her long ago.

Diane and her husband Bill did not want me in Lisa's life for fear that it would not be good for Lisa.

I respected that concern. Until his dying day Bill was always somewhat standoffish to me. It was not necessary but I was OK with it. Eventually Diane and I became friends again. Over time I would also develop a good relationship with my daughter Lisa. I often wondered how tough it was for her finding out that Bill was not her real father. I was, after all, an unknown father that came "out of the blue" to her. I am honored that she allowed me into her life. I love her as well.

Herb Koenig, my flight school friend and roommate after Vietnam and I would reunite about 15 years after we both got out of the army. For years we casually stayed in touch. Then one summer we realized that we had a special bond with each other and decided to make an annual effort to get together.

As we were both nature lovers and outdoorsmen we decided to make an annual Boundary Waters canoe area trip. Today Herb is my best friend and I consider him an older brother. We just celebrated his 70th birthday camping in the Boundary Waters.

When I was doing research to write this book I went to many Vietnam helicopter pilot and crew member reunions. This led me to reunite with Dennis Faucher, Augie Bailey, Gary Woodward, Ferrel Norman, Mike Johnson, Bernie Hernandez, Bruno Sanchez, Major Alan Jones, Ron Paye, Larry Lackey, and Bill Shillito.

Both Ferrell Norman and Mike Johnson died this year (2016) of Agent Orange related diseases. I had become close with Ferrell and miss him greatly.

Augie Bailey retired from the civil service and military as a Colonel and lives near New Orleans, LA. Today he is a paranormal investigator for the Catholic Church.

Larry Lackey was 'RIF'ed (reduction in force) from the military after Vietnam and took a lower level grade as a warrant officer to stay in the Army and continue to fly. He liked being a warrant officer better than an RLO. Today he is retired on a beautiful farm in central Georgia.

Bill Shillito retired after 20 year's of flying with the U.S. Army. Today he is the president of a telecommunications firm in North Carolina.

Dennis Faucher and I reunited at a Vietnam crew member reunion in St. Louis in 2011. We discovered that we were both searching for something that had been nagging at our souls for many years. As partner burial escort officers we have a very special bond indeed. Today Dennis is a dentist practicing in Bradford, PA. Like me, he got out of the Army after his three year commitment after flight school was up. He is the most military decorated veteran in his county.

A couple of months after the 2011 reunion in St. Louis I received a call late one evening. It was Ron Paye, the Cobra pilot that had so heroically covered us on combat assaults.

Ron had been searching for me at the request of the Shaw family. One of the attendees at the St. Louis reunion forwarded Ron my phone number. Though retired from the military, he was now affiliated with a group of veterans and patriots that had acquired and refurbished several UH-1H model Hueys.

The group called themselves American Huey 369. He had recently conducted a flyover in one of these Hueys of Lambeau Field in Green Bay, Wisconsin for the LZ Lambeau Welcome Home for Vietnam Vets in 2010.

During the ground display a family had introduced themselves to him as having lost their father/brother in Vietnam in 1972 with the 129th AHC. It was Tom Shaw Jr and his uncles Dave Shaw and Kevin Shaw. Ron immediately bonded with the Shaws and hearing that they were looking for me started a mission to find CW2 Jim Crigler.

In September of 2011 I met Tom's wife Ann, his brother Dave and wife Magali, and brother Kevin Shaw in Neillsville, WI at The Highground, one of the most special veteran memorials I have seen in the United States.

It is dedicated to all the Vietnam veterans from Wisconsin that sacrificed their lives. Each deceased Vietnam veteran has his name on a dog tag sculpture and most have their names engraved on a brick in the walking path. I arrived two hours early that day for the family meeting and took my time walking and viewing the grounds.

After about an hour I found myself walking down a brick path. I stopped to take in the breathtaking view of the fall colors in the rolling hills of this beautiful area. As I looked down I found that I was standing in front of a brick with 1LT Thomas F. Shaw engraved on it.

Amazed at this coincidence I stood there staring at the brick. Hearing footsteps walking towards me I looked up. It was Ann Shaw.

An hour later Ann, Dave, Kevin, Magzie and I were sitting in a local restaurant. I had brought with me several photos of Tom and some of his personal items that I had kept for all these years.

Kevin asked if I would consider speaking at the Catholic high school that he was president of, St. Mary's Springs which was Tom Shaw's high school as well.

It turned out that the same year that I had brought Tom back to his family from Vietnam several community and St. Mary's school members started a very special award. They called it the Tom Shaw Award. It was given to the student who best excelled in academics, sports, and community involvement. It had become, after 39 years, the most highly prized graduation award at the school. Kevin wanted me to give the Tom Shaw Award presentation speech at the 40th anniversary award in May of 2012. I was honored to do so.

Ron Paye and I became good friends. We were in fact warrior friends from long ago and had never lost that bond. Ron shared an idea that he had regarding the Shaw family.

"Most Vietnam Gold Star families do not receive the honor they deserve," he said. "I want to give the Shaw family an Honor Flight to recognize their great sacrifice to our country."

He wanted me to be his co-pilot on the flight and would let me know when American Huey 369 would be close to Wisconsin. In August of 2014 American Huey 369 conducted flight missions for a Vietnam Veterans Moving Wall event in Sheboygan, WI. I tracked down the two crew members that survived Tom Shaw and Claude Strother's crash, Bernie Hernandez and Bruno Sanchez, and flew them to Sheboygan.

That afternoon on a beautiful August day two 129th AHC pilots and the actual crew members on that fateful Vietnam mission took the Shaw family up for an Honor Flight that none of us will ever forget. It was recorded in a 6 minute mini documentary by Wisconsin Public Television. You can view it at **http://video.wpt.org/video/2365353208/** or you can simply Google "Wisconsin Life Huey Crew" and the video will show up.

Throughout my research on this book I met many Vietnam Gold Star Family members. As I mentioned earlier, their story is usually the same: they just did not talk about it due to the controversial nature of the war.

Many just suffered their grief in silence and alone. To me this just does not feel like the honor that these Americans deserve. So I made a decision many months ago to do something audacious to bring positive attention to these special families.

Starting at "Ice Out" in Northern Minnesota (this is usually the last week in April or first week in May) in 2017 I will commence a solo canoe paddle the entire length of the Mississippi river from its source in Lake Itasca, MN to the Gulf of Mexico, all 2350 miles of it.

Every paddle stroke I make will be to honor those families, and every Gold Star Family member that I meet along the way I will personally thank. With every media outlet that picks me up and every group of people that I am able to address I will share my mission. I will talk about this movement at every stop I make along this mighty river. You see to me it's the perfect main artery of this great country to speak to the heart of America. It's time to right this wrong and for me it truly is my "Mission of Honor."

PLEASE HELP ME SUPPORT THIS GREAT AMERICAN ENDEAVOR LISTED BELOW

AMERICAN HUEY 369

MISSION STATEMENT

American Huey 369 organization was formed for the specific purpose of preservation and education of the UH-1 Huey and its impact and history on the Vietnam War. Our further mission is to pay flying tribute to all veterans (especially Vietnam veterans), Gold Star Families, and all patriots. We will never forget our veterans and the Gold Star Families that have given the ultimate sacrifice for their country.

American Huey 369 is a 501(c) (3) Charitable Non-Profit organization. It operates a flying and static display (temporary) museum based in Peru, Indiana at the Grissom Aeroplex (Former Grissom AFB). We maintain three Vietnam era combat tested UH-1 Hueys. These Huey helicopters are available to participate in patriotic events such as veteran reunions, Moving Vietnam Wall or educational events, as well as veteran honor ceremonies.

www.americanhuey369.com

Why Are We in Need of a Capital Campaign?

American Huey 369 has operated for over 12 years solely on small member contributions and volunteer efforts. If we are to preserve this great flying legacy we will need to acquire enough funding to build maintenance facilities, storage hangars and general hangar facilities as well as the property to build them on. In addition we have plans for control tower facilities and a history center to include a library and educational facilities. We anticipate the total cost including upkeep to be approximately 3 million dollars and that amount will build the National American Huey History Museum!

To donate go to **www.missionofhonor.org** or the American Huey 369 website.

Thank you.

About the Author

Jim Crigler grew up in the farm country of south eastern Missouri. Graduating high school in the turbulence of 1968, Jim's goal was to be the first in his family to get a college education. A draft notice interrupted that dream.

During his four years of service in the Army, Jim served as a warrant officer helicopter pilot flying in Vietnam with A Troop 7/17 Air Cavalry and the 129th Assault Helicopter Company. Jim flew with some of the finest helicopter pilots in the world in Vietnam and personally flew thousands of combat missions during his tour of duty.

He received an honorable discharge in August of 1974 and with the help of the GI Bill graduated magna cum laude with a BS degree in Business Management from the University of Missouri.

For the last 22 years Jim has been President and CEO of Winona Search Group Inc., a human resources consulting and search firm. He lives in the woods just outside of Winona, Minnesota with his wife and two youngest daughters.